Contemporary Crafts

Decorative Beadwork

Debbie Siniska

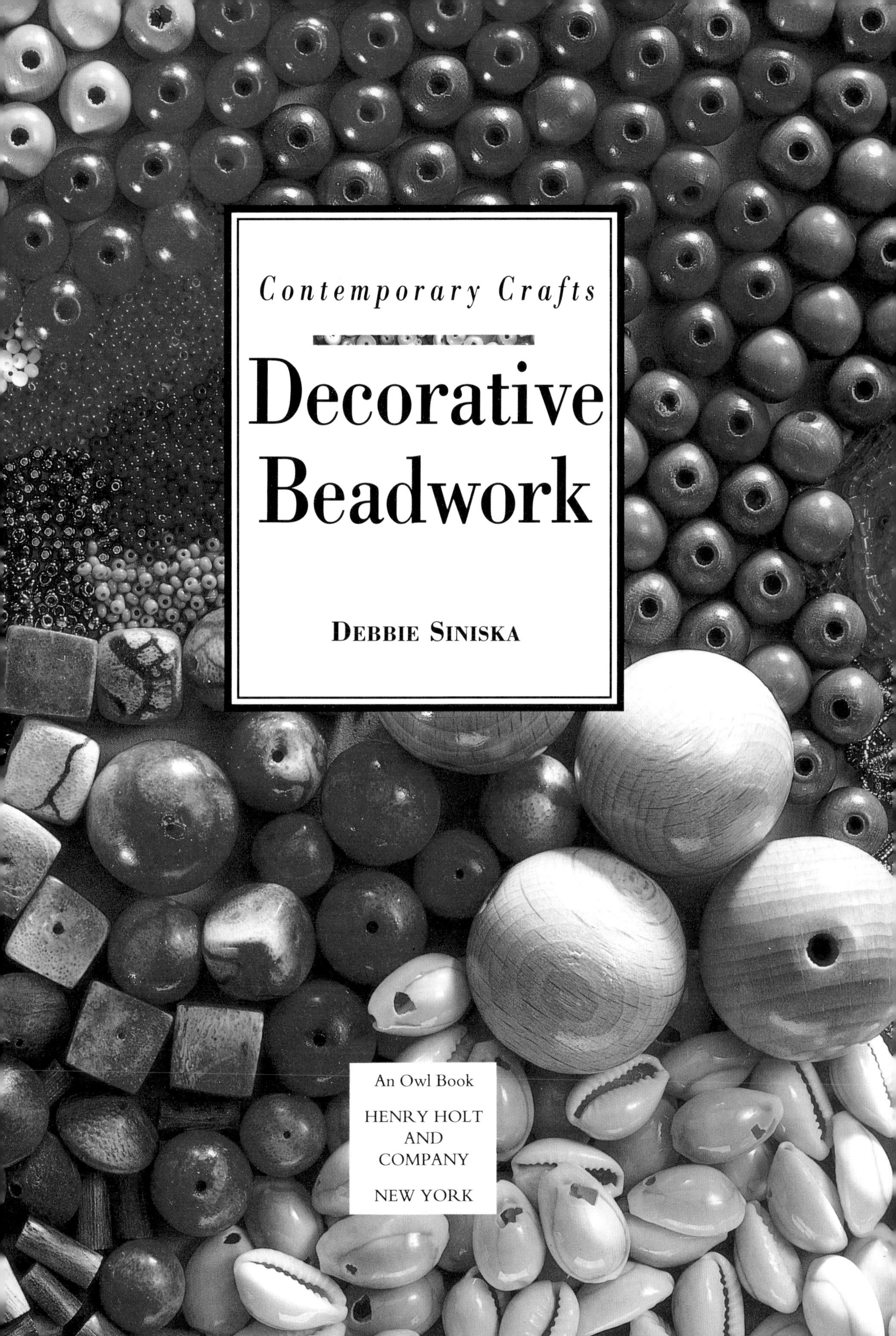

Contemporary Crafts

Decorative Beadwork

DEBBIE SINISKA

An Owl Book
HENRY HOLT AND COMPANY
NEW YORK

For Hatty Bydawell – colour was her inspiration

Henry Holt and Company, Inc.
Publishers since 1866
115 West 18th Street
New York, New York 10011

Henry Holt® is a registered
trademark of Henry Holt and Company, Inc.

First published in the United States in 1995 by
Henry Holt and Company, Inc.
Published in Canada by Fitzhenry & Whiteside Ltd.,
195 Allstate Parkway, Markham, Ontario L3R 4T8.

Originally published in England in 1994 by
Letts of London, an imprint of New Holland (Publishers) Ltd.

Library of Congress Catalog Card Number: 94-74589

ISBN 0-8050-3894-9

Henry Holt books are available for special promotions and
premiums. For details contact: Director, Special Markets.

First American/Owl Book Edition – 1995

Designed and edited by Anness Publishing Ltd.
Editorial Director: Joanna Lorenz
Project Editor: Penelope Cream
Design: Blackjacks
Photographer: Steve Tanner

Printed and bound in Singapore

1 3 5 7 9 10 8 6 4 2

CONTENTS

INTRODUCTION

BEADS HAVE PLAYED an important part in human culture throughout many civilizations. They have been used for adornment, for religion in the form of rosaries, and for their healing power; as protective charms against evil, and as visible signs of wealth and power; as currency and as methods of counting and reckoning.

Beads have been made from fossils, coral, pearls, amber, shells, wood, glass and numerous metals, including iron, gold, silver and copper.

Among old Stone Age remains, pierced teeth and shells have been found. Fossils, crinoids and ammonites, graded in size and with their natural holes enlarged, show that the manufacture of beads in their simplest forms was taking place a hundred thousand years ago. It is probable that primitive people wore beads for rituals, for their 'magic' properties and as medicines, rather than for decorative purposes. They would be worn around the neck, over the hips, through the ears and nose, and even attached to eyelashes.

Cargoes of beads were traded for ivory, animal hides, precious metals and spices by explorers all over the world, and sackfuls of beads were used to pay porters and to buy food. Native Americans ground shell by hand into smooth cylinders, which were small and looked not unlike glass. The shell, called wampum, was that of the quahog clam, and was either a deep purple-grey or white in colour, although Western wampum could also be turquoise. This 'coinage' was much prized, as the whole process of its production was difficult, and it became a symbol of wealth and status. The shell cylinders were worn as belts for prestige, and were surrendered on defeat in battle. They were used to record treaties between various tribes and, because of their great significance, were also used as peace tokens. Squaws would wear up to 200 strings of these beads on important occasions. In southern Sudan young women wore nothing but bands of beads around their waists and necks, the number of beads indicating the wealth of their fathers, and therefore their potential value as wives.

An African necklace made by the Maasai tribe from seed beads and brass

The Native Americans used the 'coin' beads as small change for silver when trading either with each other, or with the white settlers. Beads were valued at three to a penny or 360 (a fathom) to five shillings. By 1800, Crow Indians paid 100 blue beads for a horse.

The last islands to be inhabited by man, and also the last to be explored by Europeans, were the Pacific Islands, Borneo, Australia and New Zealand where the primitive currency of beads included pierced jadeite, coconut shell, seeds, whale's teeth and quartz pebbles. The most common beads were discs of polished shell and coconut. A fathom measured 1.8 metres (6 feet) and, in 1912, a quarter of a fathom of beads was equal to a shilling. One fathom would buy a good arm ring, a large pot, a club

or a spear. For 10 to 12 fathoms, you could obtain a large pig, hire a murderer, or purchase a widow! One hundred fathoms or more were necessary to atone for a murder or to buy a young girl wife. Another custom was to place 100 fathoms of beads into a netted bag as a pillow for ancestral ghosts.

Designs symbolizing the four divisions of earth are still woven into Native American bead work today, encapsulating part of a symbolic and intricate mythology and tradition that are part of their life. Zulu cultural traditions used woven belts of beads to convey messages, which would be carried by runners over vast distances to other tribes. The message would lie in the design and colours of beads used, and their relation to one another within the belt. Each colour would symbolize an emotion rather than a sentence. They were considered more important than mere adornment. Primitive Native American looms were set up by passing thread over a convenient branch, and then holding it in position with a heavy stone. Costumes would be highly decorated with beads sewn on by securing strings of beads with an overlay stitch, following a pattern. Dance collars, deerskins, buckskin dresses, horse covers, baby carriers, pipe bags, moccasins, shoulder bags, blanket strips, baby caps, purses and bags would all have been decorated in this way with beads.

By way of exchange and capture, beads subsequently found their way to other tribes, but can still be traced back to their origins. Traders and invaders from the continent also left their traces over thousands of years. Another function of beads in early trading was as a useful counting device to replace piles of stones, knots and tally sticks. The abacus is still used today in the shops and markets of Asia and, no doubt, in some schools as a way of learning to count.

A Sioux Native American belt made from glass seed beads. The colours are symbolic: turquoise represents the heavens, red the earth.

Beads have always been considered to hold special powers. Blue-glass beads were worn for good luck, and are still worn today in Arab countries by children, brides, donkeys and motor cars! Amber beads were sometimes regarded to have magical and healing properties and, in Asia, red coral and amber were used to repel lightning, tempests, whirlwinds and even witchcraft. In England, red coral was tied at the throat to stop a haemorrhage.

Shaped 'eye' beads, worn in Africa, the Middle East and Turkey, were said to protect the wearer from the 'evil eye', as the eye could look in every direction and protect from all sides. In her book, *Introducing Beads*, Mary Syed quotes a poem from Menotti's opera *Amahl and the Night Visitors:* 'In the first drawer I keep my Magic Stones, one cornelian against all evil and envy, one moonstone to make you sleep, one red coral to heal all your wounds, one lapis lazuli against quartern fever, one small jasper to help you find water, one small topaz to soothe your eyes, one red ruby to protect you from lightning. In the second drawer I keep my magic beads ... Oh, how I love all kinds of beads.'

The Chinese believed that jade held a magical quality, thought to help the dead ascend to heaven and escape the horrors of the underworld. The Egyptians buried their dead with their jewellery. Red cornelian was the colour of blood, green feldspar meant new life, while lapis lazuli denoted the colour of the heavens. Protective amulets had holes bored through them and were worn as beads.

In African cultures, beads hold great importance, and today they are worn to signify status and age. Nomadic tribes in East Africa are ordered into age sets; red and black beads are worn by 15-25 year-olds, pink and purple beads by 25-30 year-olds, and yellow beads by anyone over 30. Maasai women wear flat neck collars of beads with stripes of cowhide. Nborro (long blue beads) are for married women only, as are the beaded snuff containers which they also wear. Cowrie shells are worn to promote fertility, and tiny red seed beads are woven into the tightly braided hair of married Toposa women.

The religious significance of beads has also been revered by many cultures. Bede is an Anglo-Saxon word meaning 'bidden to pray' and beaded rosaries were used along the prayer wheels in medieval Britain. Rosaries were made up of knots or beads; the beads would be slipped through the fingers to be counted or 'told' in the dark, and each bead would represent a prayer. Moslems used 99 beads to pray to Allah, and, in the Middle East, 33 amber beads were used as a rosary and also as worry beads. Tibetan Buddhist monks used nuts or seeds or carved human bone for the same purpose. Perfumed rosary beads were sometimes made of a paste of finely chopped rose petals, which turned hard and black when dry. Nutmeg, coffee beans and cloves were also used. The scented beads had a dual use when water or washing was scarce. Eighteenth-century Austrian 'need beads' were also a form of rosary, and magical strings of oddments were carried or worn to protect children from sickness and the evil eye.

The purely decorative quality of beads has always been an important part of their history, but, even when used as ornaments, beads have still been an indication of a person's status, or used to convey a certain message. In medieval Europe, and in England, for example, laws and decrees proclaimed that only certain classes of society could wear particular categories of jewellery.

Beads have a long and fascinating history, and their fascination continues to the present day. They are now available in an immense range of both natural and man-made materials, and in every size, shape and colour imaginable. Even inexpensive beads can be used to create wonderful pieces of jewellery, weaving or other beadwork, making them accessible to all, and the advent of plastics has opened up even more possibilities. The only restriction to what can be done with beads is the worker's creative imagination!

A fringed Victorian purse woven from tiny steel beads. The drawstring and the slots it passes through would have been worked in while weaving was in progress.

Materials and Equipment

THE MATERIALS AND EQUIPMENT needed for working with beads are readily available from specialist and craft shops, department stores and by mail order (see the list of Suppliers on page 94). The basic items that you will require are listed here; individual projects give details of specific materials and equipment.

BEADS

A vast range of beads is available today, in a wide variety of shapes, sizes and colours. Beads are made from many materials, both natural and man-made, including wood, bone, shell, ivory, mother-of-pearl, plastic, glass, seeds, cork, paper, brass, steel, precious metals, precious or semi-precious stones and even finely woven horse hair. Small glass rocaille (seed) beads are very popular and come in many colours and different finishes, including metallic and iridescent. The quality of rocaille beads, which come from all over the world, does vary, although this may not always matter. Japanese rocailles are the most even in size, and will suit several of the projects in the book. Bugle beads are also very useful. These are long cylindrical beads which come in varying lengths, and with either a smooth or an attractive faceted finish.

It is wise to select beads of even size, and with good open holes, to enable a needle and thread to pass through them easily several times. You will find yourself doing this especially when ending off a piece of work. If you have to force a needle through a small hole, it will shatter the bead, perhaps cut the thread, and may even snap your needle. Experience will teach you whether a needle can be pulled through a bead, and you can use pliers to pull a needle clear if the fit is tight. Never use your teeth!

Look out for old beads when scouting round jumble sales and charity shops. Old necklaces often have fittings which can be re-used, some of which may be quite ornate. Undo any strings of beads very carefully that you may find in this way. If the beads have wire through them, it may be better to leave them like this, and to incorporate them into some other project. Put all your beads into glass jars or clear plastic containers, so that you can see at a glance exactly what you have.

THREADS

NYLON-MONOFILAMENT FISHING LINE: this can be used for many types of beadwork. It is strong and transparent, and has a little give in it, making the work hard-wearing. Nylon thread is smooth, however, and if the ends are not properly worked in, they may come loose, so always take care when starting and finishing off this thread. Strong cotton thread, used double, is more suitable for a beaded fringe, which will hang stiffly if worked on nylon thread but, for most purposes, this monofilament is a good choice. Use 1.5-1.8 kg ($3\frac{1}{2}$-4 lb) breaking strength when working with small rocailles. You may find that you need to flatten the end of the nylon between your teeth in order for it to pass through the eye of the needle.

THICKER NYLON THREAD: this can be used with a needle when stringing lengths of large beads. It should be knotted at the start and finish of the work, and some people also like to singe the ends to secure them more fully.

FINE BONDED-NYLON THREAD: this is similar to very strong, fluid cotton or button thread, and can be strengthened by running through beeswax. This will also help to prevent tangles. This type of thread is ideal for threading up a bead loom. The finished weaving will hang softly, and an added fringe on the end of a loomed strip will be fluid and full of movement.

COTTON-COVERED SHIRRING ELASTIC: this can be used to thread up a loom, or for any beaded item requiring flexibility (such as a hair ornament) and is easy to manipulate, making it particularly useful for a beginner. It can also be threaded through the eye of a needle, by threading the needle first with a small, double length of cotton, placing the pulled-out covering threads of the elastic through the loop of the doubled cotton thread, and then pulling the elastic through.

BEAD LOOMS

There are various types of commercially made bead looms. The best kind has rollers at each end, which can be tightened or loosened with wing nuts. This allows a long piece of beading to be worked, winding it on to one of the rollers. (A pad of cloth or cardboard can be positioned over the pin so that the wound-on weaving will be protected.)

The bead loom used for the woven bag panel and watchstrap projects on pages 61 and 91 of this book was made to order and both the 7.5 cm (3 in) and the wider 15 cm (6 in) looms are available from Debbie Siniska (see the list of Suppliers on page 95). The wider loom accommodates fairly broad strips of beading, or takes several narrower strips at a time. There are three pins for tying off the work, on the rollers.

If you wish to experiment with bead weaving before buying a proper loom, it is possible to make a bead loom from odd pieces of wood. Take a flat piece of wood, with two oblong blocks at either end. Nail panel pins (finishing nails) along each block, at equal intervals, but not directly opposite one another. The warp threads are then wound around the pins (nails). As these are raised on blocks, your hands will pass freely underneath when working.

NEEDLES

Special beading needles can be purchased from specialist bead shops or craft shops (see the list of Suppliers on page 94). These needles are long and fine, and will enable you to pick up several beads at a time. They also have long, fine eyes which take the thread easily. Alternatively, you can make your own needles with fine fuse wire. Simply bend a short length of the wire in half and twist it, leaving a loop at the end through which the thread can pass.

Beading needles are perfectly usable if they become bent which, because they are so fine, does tend to happen after a short time in use. These needles do sometimes snap, however, particularly when being used by a beginner as there is a tendency to grip the needle too firmly.

If the beads are able to take a larger needle, this is quite acceptable. Your favourite needle may be a little easier to thread, but it will not have the length of a beading needle, restricting the number of beads that you can pick up at one time.

If you are planning to incorporate beads in knitting, first pass some cotton over the yarn, then thread the two cotton ends through the eye of the needle, and pull the yarn through. Your beads can then be threaded on to the yarn. Keep a pincushion at hand in which to stick the needle when it is not in use. Try to make this a habit, in order to avoid the problem of lost needles.

METAL FASTENERS

Some projects in this book have all-bead fasteners, which are often more appropriate to the finished item, but there are also several other types of suitable fastenings or findings (the metal components used for making jewellery). Bolt rings and split rings, screw 'torpedo' clasps, hooks and eyes, press studs, Velcro (for belts) and fine ribbon or cord can also be used as fastenings. All these fastenings are widely available from specialist and craft shops (see the list of Suppliers on page 94).

JEWELLERY FINDINGS

Various types of ear wire for pierced ears are available, made of either pure metals or other base metals. All have a small loop which can be fitted on to an earring, using pliers. Various clip-on fittings are also available, either to screw on to the ear or to spring shut.

The most common type of fastening for necklaces and bracelets uses a bolt ring at one end, with a sprung catch, and a split ring at the other. Screw clasps are also useful. Both types of fastening are easily attached using the threads at the ends of the piece of beadwork.

TAPE MEASURE

This is a useful piece of equipment for working with beads. To make a measure that will not slip about, place two pins in a tablecloth on your working part of the table, or in a cloth on your work surface, spaced apart at the required width. Alternatively, mark a piece of cardboard to use as a rigid measure, or use a yardstick.

SCISSORS

Always keep a small pair of sharp, pointed scissors to hand when beading, and never break thread by snapping it with your fingers, or biting it with your teeth. If tiny ends of nylon are left sticking out of a piece

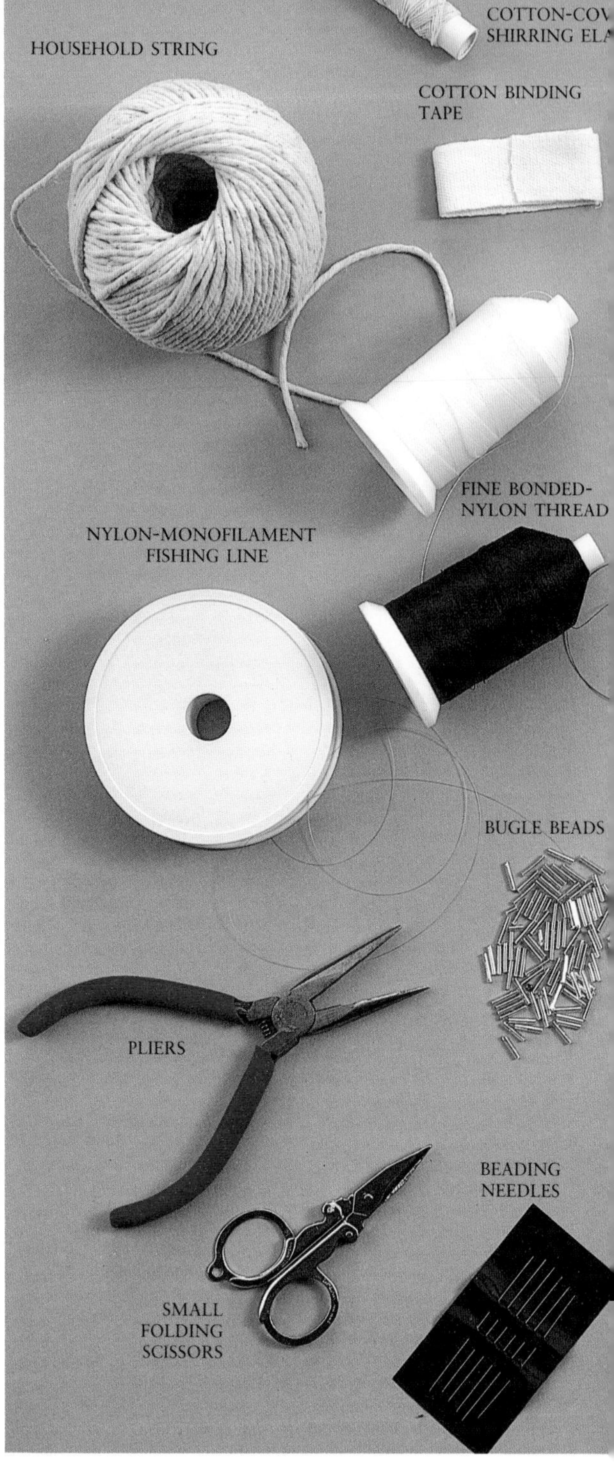

of work they will really prick, so use a pair of curved nail scissors to snip ends close to the beadwork.

PLIERS

A small pair of blunt-nosed or pointed pliers is useful for easing a needle through an awkward turn, or for pinching out and smashing an unwanted bead in a piece of glass beadwork. Be *very* careful not to damage the working

thread if you have to resort to this method. An alternative technique is to place a very fat needle in the hole of an unwanted bead, lie it on a flat surface and tap it with a hammer to smash the bead. A new one can then be worked in its place.

WORKING BOARD OR MAT

This piece of equipment can be made from a thick piece of polystyrene (styrofoam), which is then covered with wadding (batting) and fabric. This will enable you to pin work down to a secure base while working with two needles, or simply to manoeuvre the work with greater ease. You can also use a quilted mat or cushion to bead on your lap. Work at a table covered with a cloth, so that the beads will not scatter too far if spilled. You can carry your beadwork project from room to room on a tray which has handles and a lip around the edge.

Basic Techniques

THIS BOOK TAKES YOU through 12 projects, showing ways in which to construct jewellery, how to create both simple surface beading and more elaborate designs, and how to use traditional and contemporary techniques. The basic techniques for working with beads are explained here.

THREADING UP A BEAD LOOM

When threading up a bead loom, always use one more warp thread than the number of beads you require across the width of your weaving. (Warp threads are the threads that come downward over the spacers, through which the weft threads are woven.)

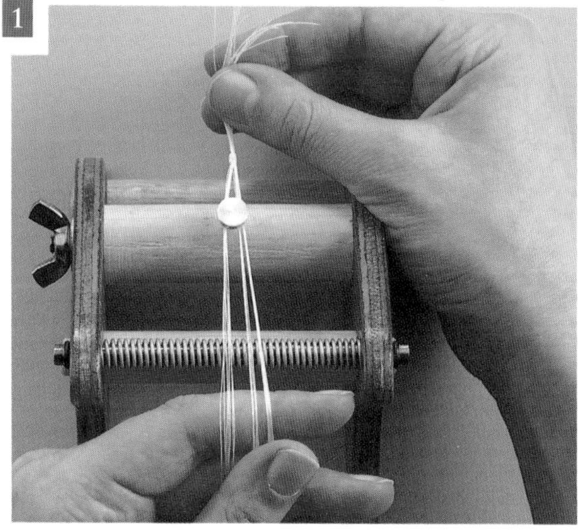

1 Cut the required number of lengths of fluid, bonded-nylon thread, or any other strong thread, so that they are at least 30-38 cm (12-15 in) longer than the finished project will be. This will allow for ending off the work properly (see page 18). Tie these lengths into a knot at one end, and place the threads on either side of the pin on the roller. The knot should sit directly behind the pin. Make sure that the wing nut is tightened, so that the roller does not slip around.

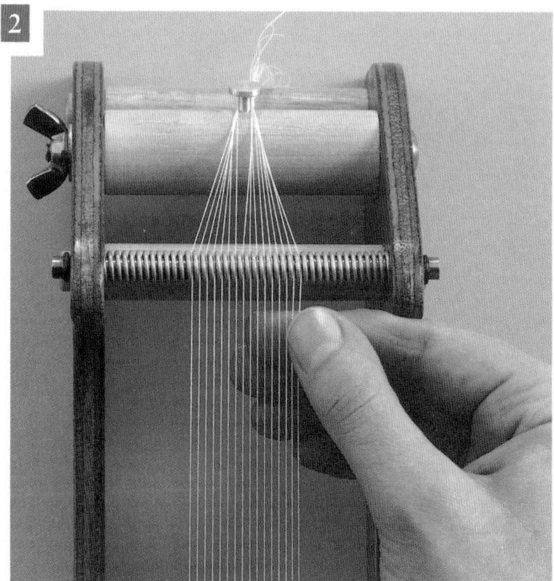

2 Lay the threads over the spacers, making sure that each one lies between the grooves of the coil. Bring the threads down to lie in the grooves of the spacers at the other end, being sure to hold them evenly between an outstretched forefinger and middle finger. Try to keep this grip on the threads throughout the whole process of winding on.

3 To wind the threads on to the roller furthest away from you, first loosen the wing nut on this roller. With your right hand, grip the roller and slowly wind it away from you, using your left hand to maintain an even hold on the threads nearest to you. Make sure that the knot end always lies behind the pin, and that the ends are not trapped under the threads being wound on to the roller. Flick these ends free if necessary with a small pair of closed, pointed scissors.

When you have finished winding on, tighten both wing nuts, still holding the warp threads, and then tie the free ends around the roller nearest to you. You can adjust the tension at this point by using the wing nuts to tighten or loosen the warp threads. The threads should be taut, so that they 'ping' when tested with a finger.

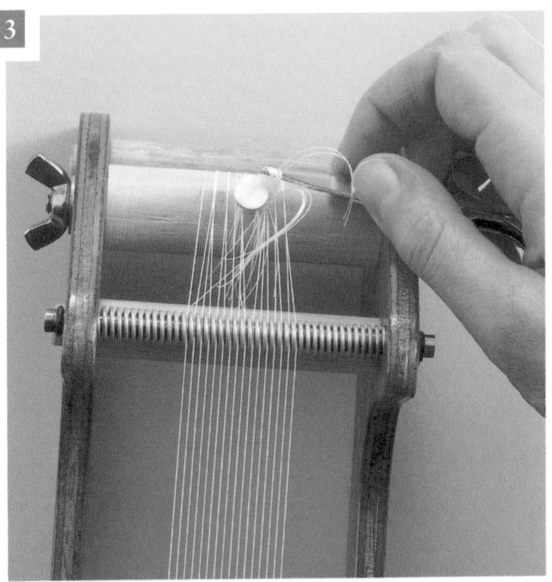

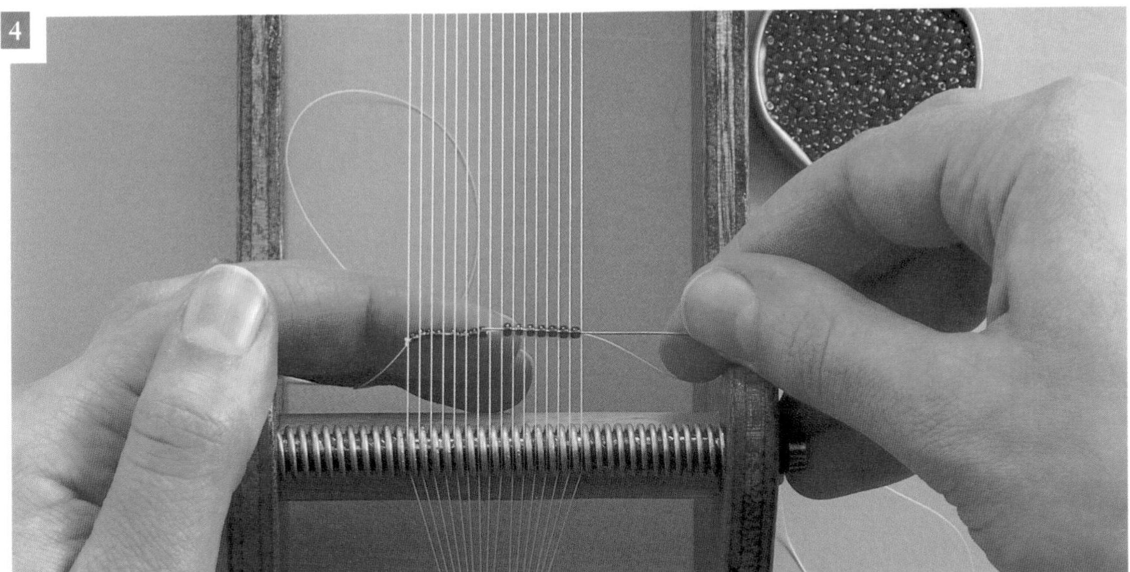

4 To begin weaving, take an open-arm's length of thread, thread up a needle and tie the thread on to the left-hand warp, at a point approximately 2.5 cm (1 in) away from the roller. Leave an end long enough to thread into a needle once the weaving is complete, in order to secure it. Always tie on the thread using two knots.

Now take the thread *under* the warp threads to the right side, and pick up your beads. Let them fall up to the knot, and push them up between the warp threads. With the needle in your right hand, take it through the beads, making sure that it passes *over* the warps. Watch for the glint of needle, between each bead, as you make this manoeuvre.

For the following row, simply take the thread through to the left side, pulling the beads into place. Take the thread *under* the warps to the right-hand side, and pick up the next group of beads. Continue in this manner until the weaving is complete.

ENDING OFF LOOMED WORK

One method of ending off loomed work is first to tie off the threads as above, and then to thread on larger beads. You can do this on double-warp ends, braiding or knotting the threads between the beads.

Alternatively, if you are making a wall panel, you can make a hanging fringe at the bottom edge of the weaving. To make a fringe, thread up each (or every other) warp with a needle and thread on rocailles, pass around the last bead, and take the needle up the row of beads which forms the fringe strands. Finally, take the needle and thread back into the weaving to end off neatly.

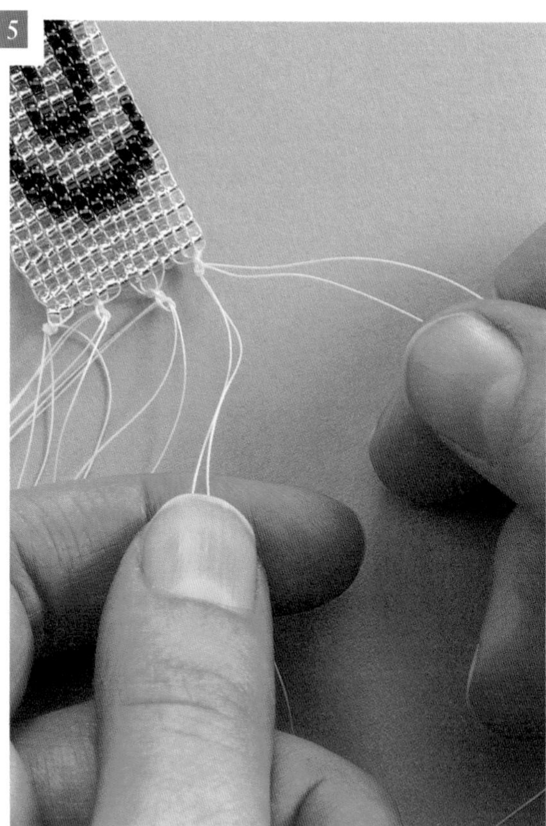

5 To end off a piece of woven beadwork, carefully cut the completed strip from the loom, leaving the warp threads sufficiently long to enable you to tie them off. Tie pairs of thread ends together with double knots to secure the weaving.

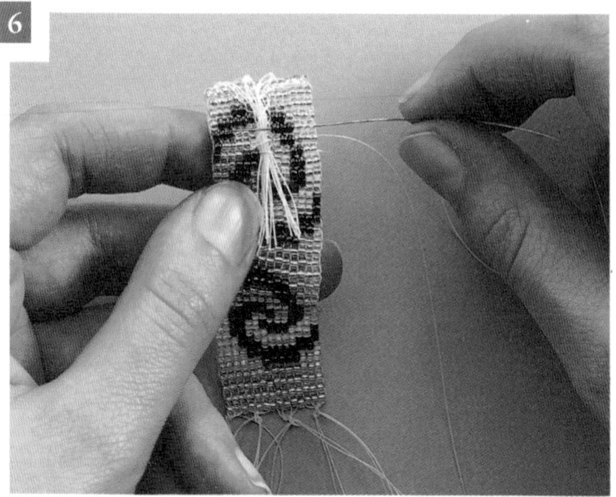

6 Lay these knotted warp threads flat along the surface at each end of the weaving. Bring a new thread into the beads, securing it with a knot, and oversew the warp threads to the weaving, working the thread through several rows.

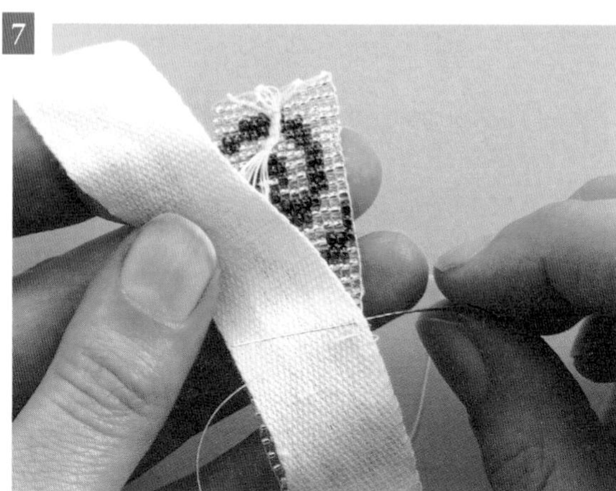

7 Cut a piece of cotton binding tape long enough to cover the weaving, plus a small hem at either end. Oversew the binding tape neatly to the back of the weaving with sewing thread, catching the stitches on the edge warp threads and turning under the tape at each end.

STARTING BEADWORK

When starting a piece of beadwork, always knot around the first bead. If you are using single thread, pass through the eye of the needle, take it through the bead, and knot the thread securely. Do this twice before

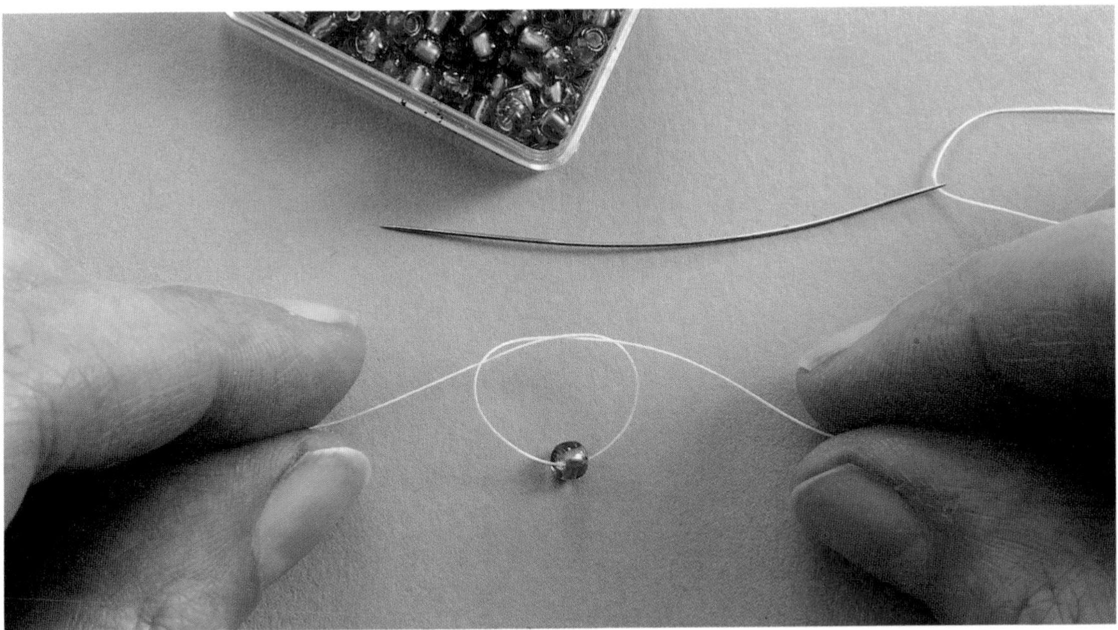

To start off, tie the thread securely on to the first bead

proceeding with the beadwork. If using double thread, thread on the needle and knot the ends of the thread together. Thread on the first bead, then bring the needle back over the bead and between the two threads to secure.

As described earlier, it is always advisable to leave a thread end of approximately 30-38 cm (12-15 in), which can be woven back through the work afterwards. This will give it added strength.

A thread end from the weaving can also be used to attach a fastening, eliminating the need to join on a new thread. The advantage of using a new thread to attach fastenings, however, is that the work will not be in danger if the fastening should happen to come loose.

If you are working with cotton-covered shirring elastic, do not be tempted to use too long a piece of thread (an arm's length is quite sufficient), as it will fray and is also liable to knot up on itself. Be sure to snip the fraying ends frequently when working.

When using tiny beads, and working a tiny pattern, it is sometimes awkward to hold the work at the beginning. A working board, to which the work can be pinned (see page 15) is useful for this purpose and will enable you to see exactly what you are doing. A pencil can be used to hold a beaded tube as it is being worked.

ENDING OFF BEADWORK

As a general rule, when finishing work or joining on a new thread, find an appropriate place in the pattern at which to stop. Knot the working thread on the thread of the work you have done, and the knot will slip inside the beads. (If you knot around a bead, it will drag the work.) Take the thread end back through the work, knotting at intervals on the thread, as far back into the work as you feel is necessary to create a secure finish.

JOINING ON A NEW THREAD

To join on a new thread, work it up through the beadwork, coming out at the point at which you ended the previous thread. You can mark this point by securing a piece of cotton in the relevant position when ending off. Bring out the new thread at exactly this point, secure it and then remove the marking cotton.

MAKING AND ATTACHING A FASTENING BEAD

A covered fastening bead is used in combination with a beaded loop to fasten a piece of weaving. It can match the work exactly, if you cover the bead with the same beads used for the weaving. A light wooden bead, approximately the size of a pea, is the best type to use as a base for covering with small rocaille beads. Try to find a wooden bead with a good-sized hole that is large enough to take several passings of thread.

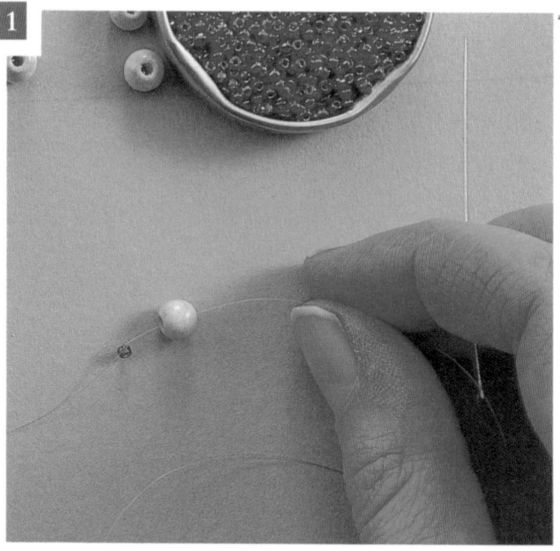

1 To make a covered bead, take a single-arm's length of thread and knot on the first rocaille (see 'Starting Beadwork' on page 19), leaving a 'tail' of approximately 25 cm (10 in). Next, thread on the wooden bead to be covered.

2 Pick up several rocailles (the exact number will depend on the size of the wooden bead) and pass the needle back up through the base bead to complete the first 'cover' row.

3

3 Repeat this process until the base bead is covered with rocailles.

When using a covered fastening bead, always attach this to the piece of work before you make the loop (see overleaf), so that you can 'test' the fit of loop over the bead before completing the fastening. The weaving to which the fastening is to be attached should be properly ended off using one of the two methods described in this section.

4

The covered bead will have emerging from it the long 'tail' that you left at the beginning and the working thread, which you will use to sew the fastening to the end of the work. This thread will be coming out at the bottom of the covered bead.

4 To attach the fastening, pick up five or six rocaille beads, take the needle into the centre bead of the top row of the weaving and along the beads, out to the edge. Take the needle back along the next row of beads to the other side, then pass the needle back through the beads in the top row, to the centre bead but one. Pick up five or six rocailles for the 'stem' and take the thread up into the covered fastening bead. Repeat this process several times with the needle and thread to make a secure end.

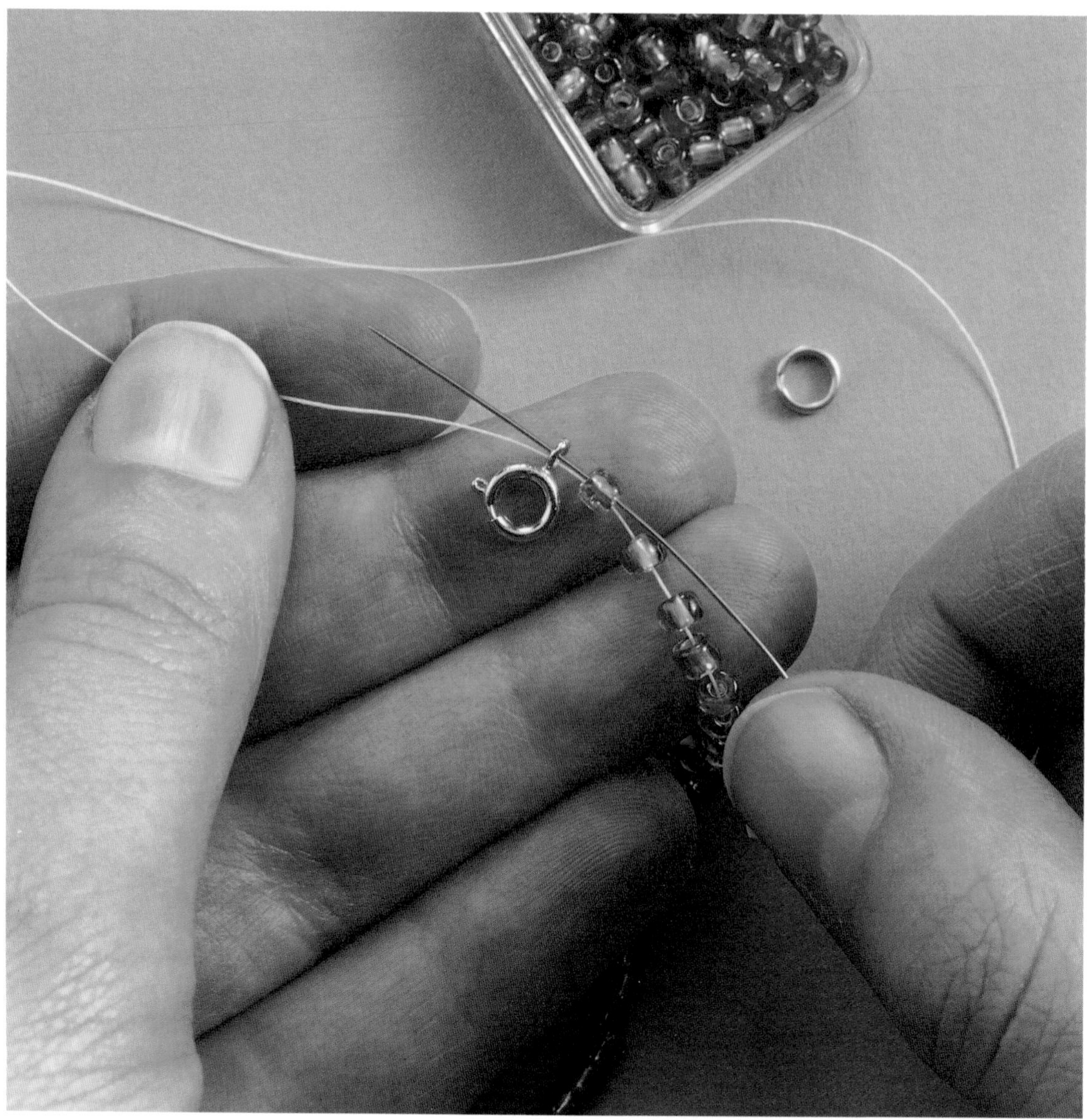

When attaching a bolt-ring fastening, take the thread through two or three times to secure properly.

ATTACHING JEWELLERY CLASPS AND FASTENINGS

When attaching a clasp to a necklace or bracelet, two or three knots will suffice. Try to resist the temptation to make a lot of knots, as they will look ugly on the finished work.

Some bolt rings have a break in the part that is attached to the necklace or bracelet. When sewing this type of clasp to the end of a piece of work, you should therefore take the thread around the second part of the bolt ring two or three times before knotting, to make sure that the fastening cannot fall off through the break in the fitting.

MAKING AND ATTACHING A FASTENING LOOP

For the fastening loop at the other end of the work, thread up a new thread on to the needle, and run it into the work, five or six rows down.

When making a loop fastening, pass the thread through the loop several times for a secure finish.

Knot the thread here and there and bring it out at the end of the weaving. Pick up as many rocailles as are needed (test this by passing the loop over the covered bead at the opposite end of the work). The loop should sit neatly in the centre of the top edge of the weaving. Pass the thread back and forth through the loop and the top few rows of weaving to create a firm finish.

GENERAL WORKING TIPS

- To create an even tension in your beadwork, always pull the working thread gently but firmly in the direction in which it is going.
- When taking thread ends back through finished work, knotting here and there for a secure finish, do not pull the knots too tightly, as this will make the work stiff and uneven.
- Roll woven beads between a thumb and forefinger to make them lie more evenly.
- Never use glue on bead jewellery, as it is messy and will never be completely secure. The ends of nylon thread can be singed with a match flame but, if the thread is worked through properly, this will not be necessary. Any binding tape or fastenings must be sewn on to the beadwork.
- When picking up beads on a needle, pile the beads up together in a shallow saucer. This will enable you to feed in the needle by scooping up the beads from one side in a horizontal movement. Alternatively, if you are a beginner, you may prefer to pick up each bead with a thumb and forefinger before pushing the needle through.
- Read through all the instructions carefully and have all the necessary materials at hand before starting a project.

GALLERY

THE MANY TYPES of beads available today offer an almost endless source of inspiration to those who work with them. From intricate jewellery designs composed of tiny rocaille beads to large-scale pieces made in bold, bright colours, the items shown in this section reveal just some of the many techniques and working methods in use today.

Ideas for these pieces have come from many different origins, including traditional and contemporary designs, illustration and the natural world. Look out for unusual and interesting beads wherever you go, and make use of their potential to create your own unique beadwork.

~

Aqua and Pearl Earrings
FRANCES BENDIXSON
Earrings made of silver wire and aquamarine, mother-of-pearl, pearl, ivory, gold and silver beads.

Celtic Hanging and Sampler

JEAN GROWNEY

The hanging is woven on a beadloom and its warp threads are intricately knotted and fringed. The beads in the sampler were back-stitched on to base material following a pattern.

. . . .

Child's Hat

LINDY RICHARDSON

This sequined hat is crowned with an intricately beaded fabric bird, complete with rocaille head plumes and tail feathers.

. . . .

Fringed Face Hanging

DEBBIE SINISKA

This is composed of three separate woven rocaille sections which can be hung together or apart. The warp threads are used to form the heavy beaded fringing.

Bead and Wire Jewellery

DIANA LAURIE

This collection of jewellery is made from an exotic mixture of beads of different materials. The beads are held together by strong wire in a mass of colour.

Glass Beads

AXEL RUSSMEYER

These beautifully constructed beads are covered in miniature antique rocailles, old French metal beads and cut steel beads. They can be strung together as necklaces or worn as cuff-links, buttons and earrings.

. . . .

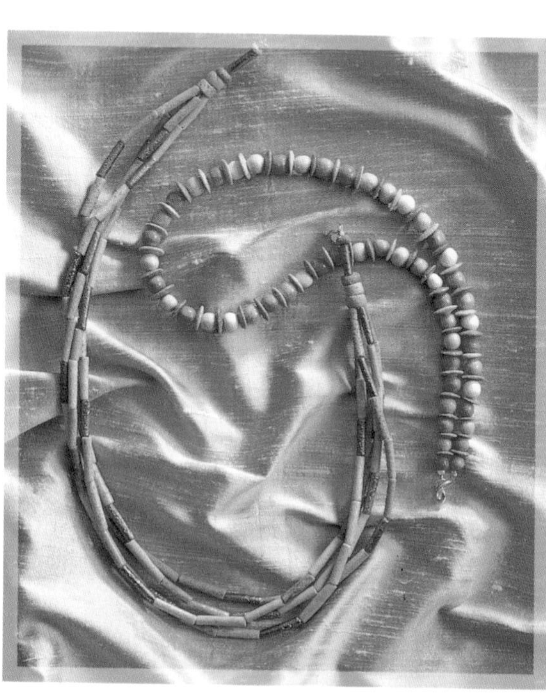

Egyptian Paste Beads

SOPHIE MILBURN

These necklaces are constructed from Egyptian paste, a soda-based clay. The longer beads are hollow, rolled around newspaper which burns away when fired.

. . . .

Wire and Glass Earrings
DIANA LAURIE
Simple loop earrings made from coloured glass beads connected by brass and silver wire.

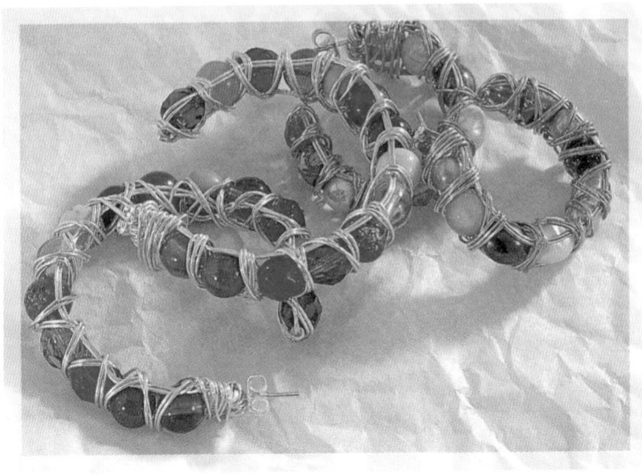

Magnifying Glass
FRANCES BENDIXSON
A pendant magnifier made with a simple strand of silver wire threaded through quartz crystal beads.

Necklace and Earrings
JANET COLES BEAD EMPORIUM

These are made to traditional Maasai design using porcupine quills and coconut shell discs. The necklace also has a bone batik bead formed from bone plugged with wood. Wax is dribbled on to this bead, which is dyed black, and then removed to produce a two-colour effect.

Pearl and Diamante Collection
DIANA WILSON

This elegant ensemble is made from pearls and diamante-inlaid beads. The stringing technique demonstrates the versatility of multiple-tier patterns.

Beadwork Cushion
EVELYN COHEN
This cushion is made from mixed rocaille beads embroidered on to silk and backed with velvet. It is trimmed with decorative fringed loops.

Trade Beads
KOUADIO N'GUESSAN
These traditional African trade beads were originally used as a form of currency in West Africa. Kouadio's work uses predominantly antique glass beads contrasted in various patterns and colour schemes.

Chevron-Pattern Earrings

In beadwork, the simplest designs are often the most effective. Here, a combination of tiny rocaille beads and long bugle beads in classic silver and black makes an exotic pair of earrings. The hanging bead strands are full of movement, and the bugles really sparkle as they catch the light. The beauty of these earrings is that, although they are fairly large, they are very light in weight, making them comfortable to wear. The design can easily be adapted to make the earrings longer or shorter as desired.

~

MATERIALS AND EQUIPMENT

• *fine bonded-nylon thread* • *scissors* • *fine beading needle* • *silver bugle beads* • *small silver and black rocaille beads (or 2 colours of your choice)* • *2 earring wires* • *pliers*

......

1 Take an open-arm's length of thread, and thread up the needle. Pick up two bugle beads, and let them fall to the middle of the thread. Pass the needle back down through the first bugle, pulling the thread to leave an end measuring approximately 30 cm (12 in). This end can be worked back into the beads when you have completed the earring.

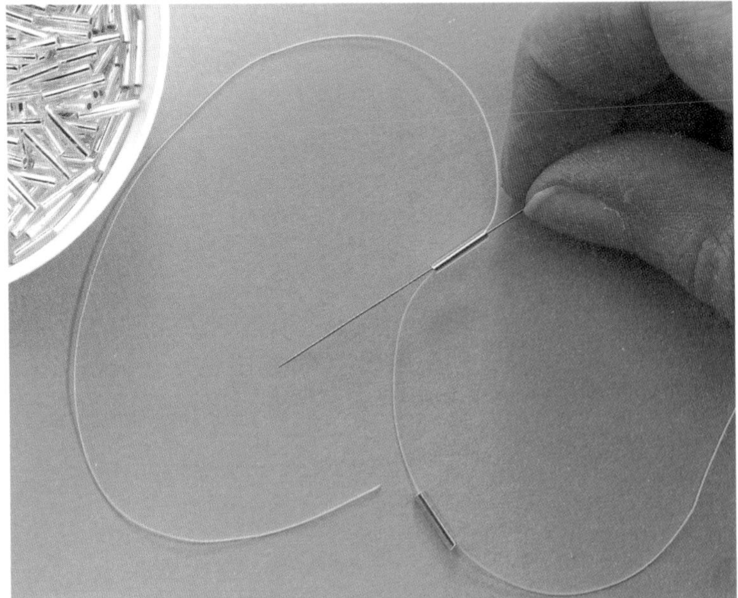

2 Take the needle back up through the second bugle, and draw the two beads together.

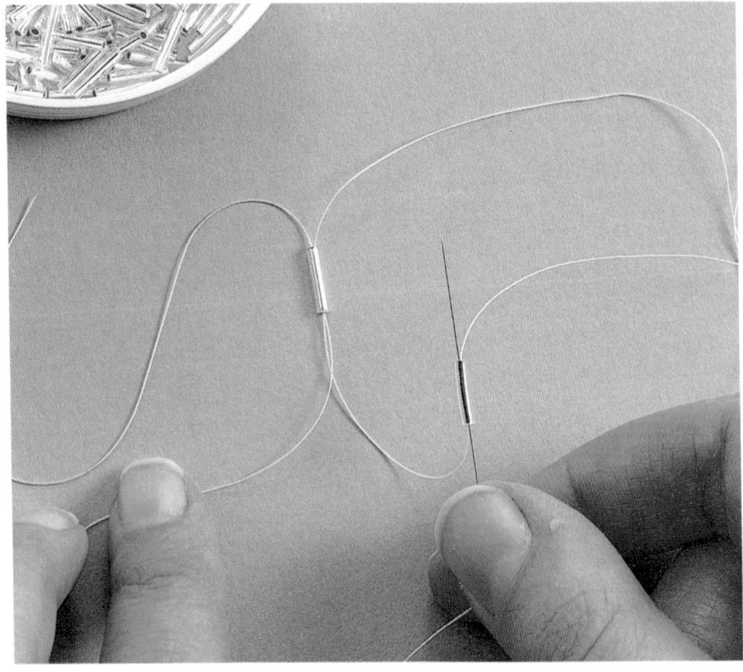

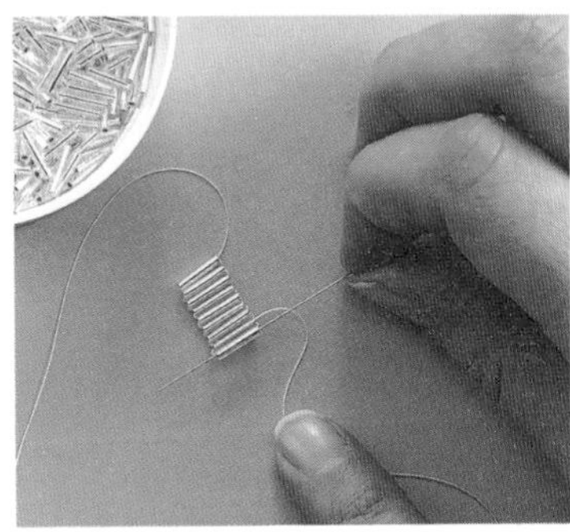

3 Continue adding beads in this way until you have a total of nine bugles strung side by side.

4 To secure this 'base' line, take the needle back and forth through each bugle once again, until you have reached the first bead. The needle will come out at the opposite end of the first bugle from which you began, with the starting thread emerging from the other end.

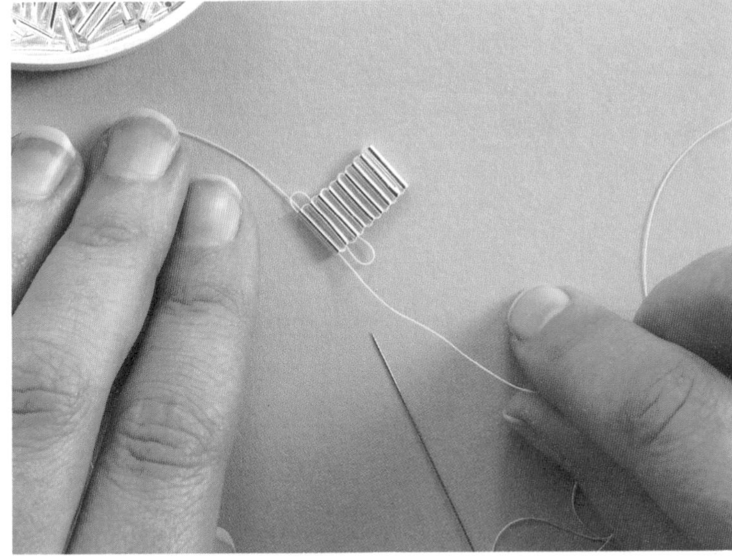

5 Pick up the first black rocaille bead on the needle, and let it fall to the base of the thread. Take the needle through the first loop of thread lying between the row of bugles.

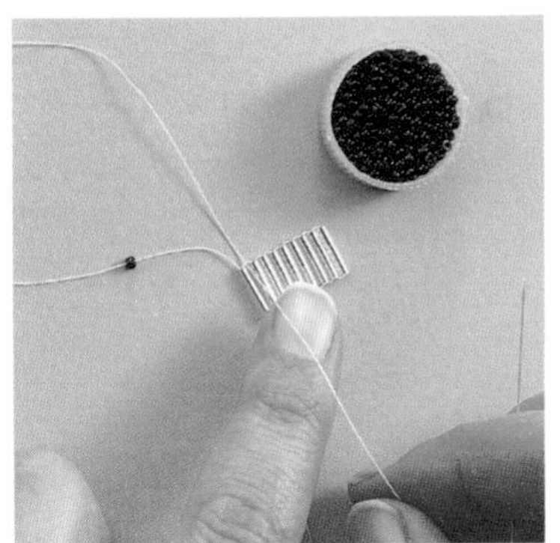

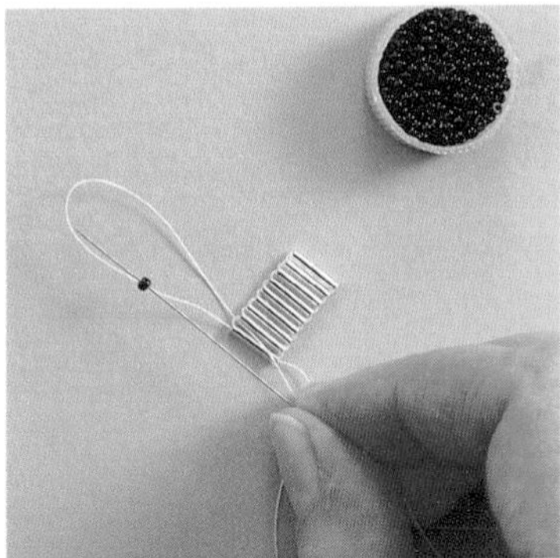

6 Pass the needle back up through this first rocaille, and draw the thread through until the rocaille is sitting on top of the bugle beads.

7 Pick up and thread on alternate silver and black rocailles in the same way until you have completed the first row. To make the second row, you will be securing each rocaille on the thread loops of the first row. The number of beads will naturally decrease in number as each row is formed to make a pyramid shape.

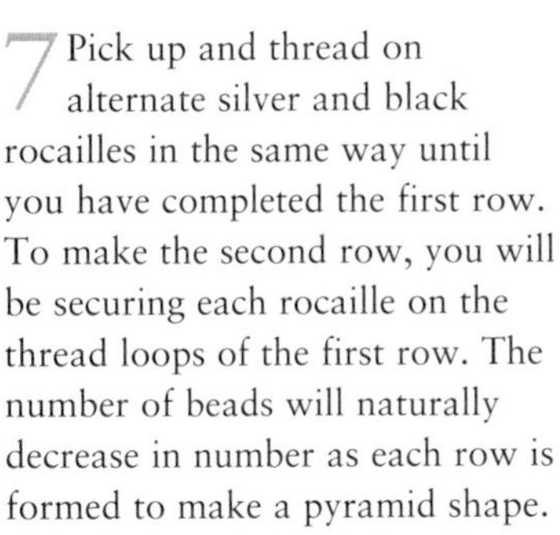

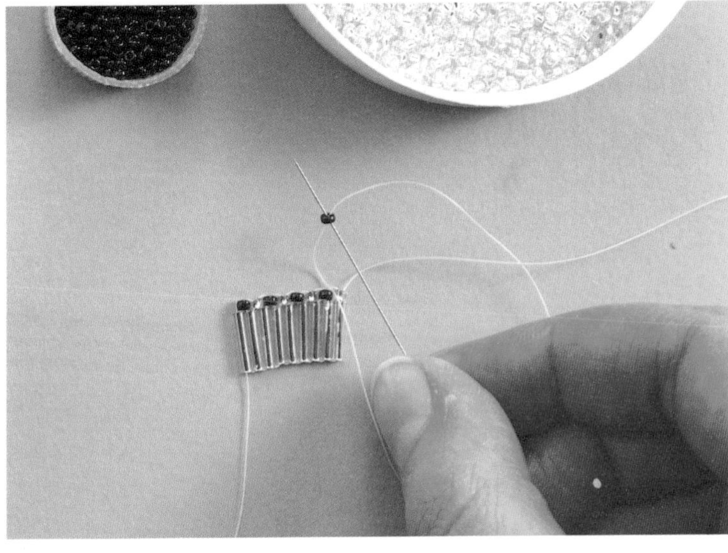

8 Having created the pyramid shape, finishing with a single rocaille in the top row, make a loop on which the earring wire will be attached. Pick up four rocaille beads (two of each colour) and let them fall to the base of the thread. Take the needle through these rocailles a second time, and pull the loop closed.

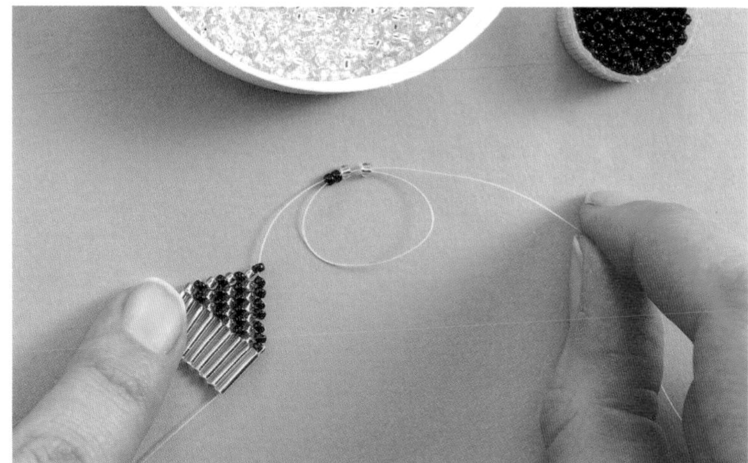

9 Take the needle down through the outer beads that form one side of the pyramid shape.

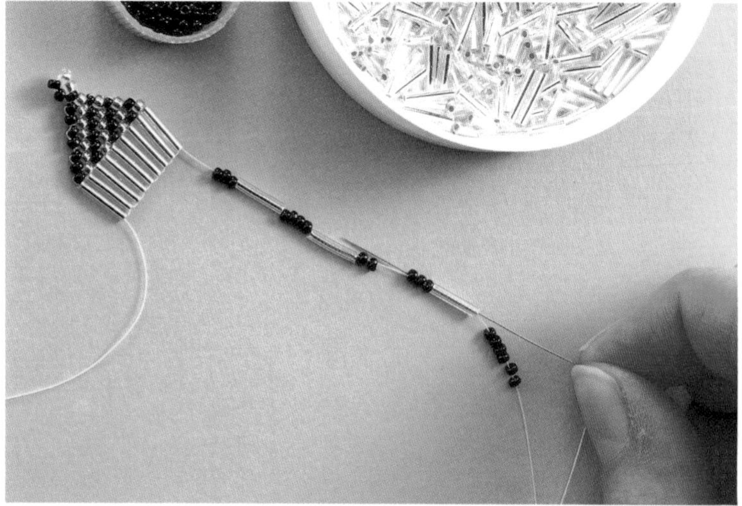

10 Take the needle down through the end bugle. In order to form the fringed part of the earring, first pick up your chosen sequence of beads. To form a pretty end on the strand, pick up the last six rocailles and pass the thread back through the next bugle in line, back up the whole first row, and into the first bugle of the base row.

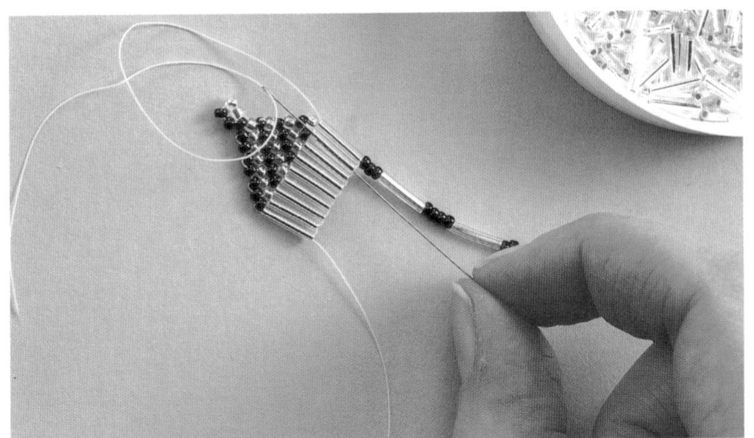

11 To form the next strand of the fringe, first pass the thread down through the next base bugle bead, ready to thread on the next strand.

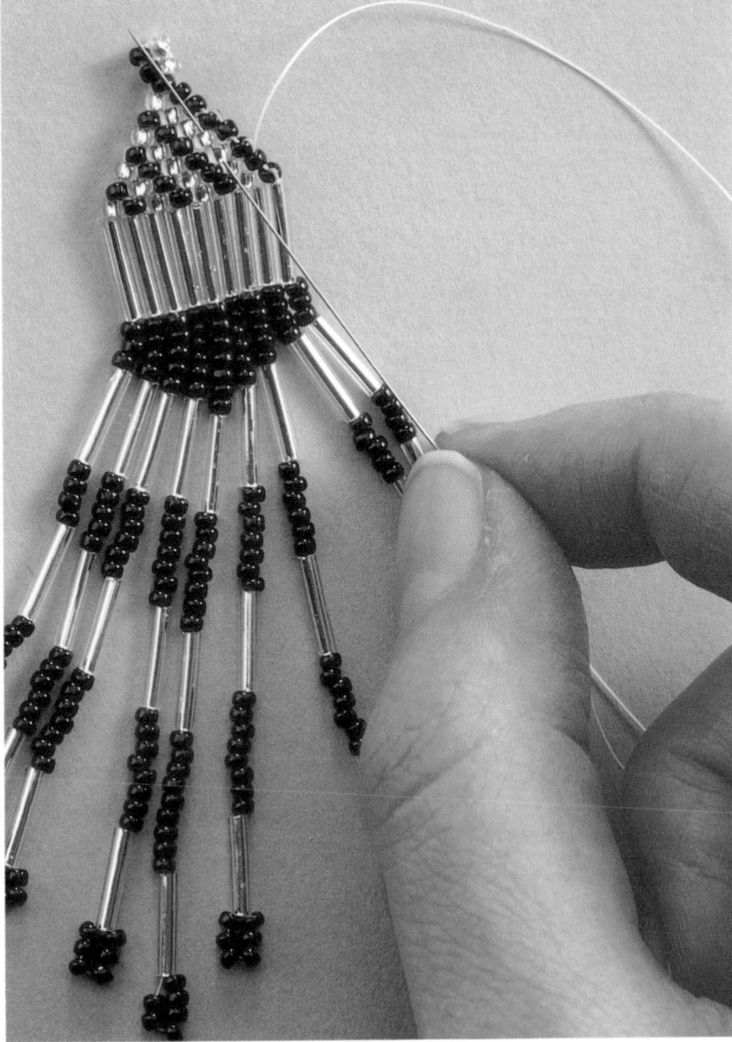

12 For your nine base bugle beads, you will have nine fringe strands – be creative and make the pattern as attractive as you can. The V-shaped pattern shown here is easily made. Simply pick up one extra rocaille bead in each section of rocailles, until you reach the centre line, and then reverse the sequence. When you have completed all nine strands, work the thread back into the earring and snip the thread close. Work in the other thread that was left at the beginning.

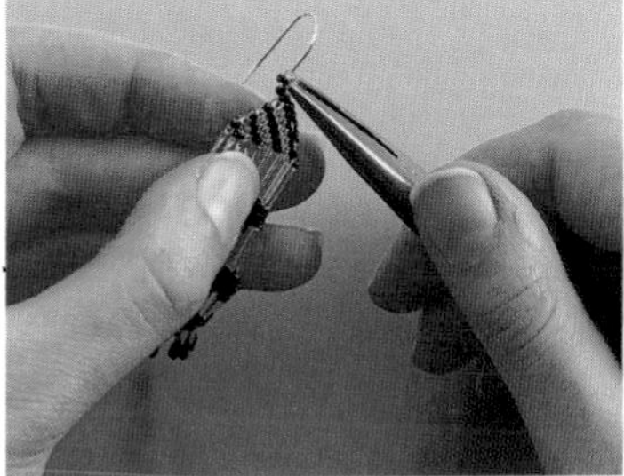

13 Hook an earring wire through the beaded loop at the top of the earring, and pinch the wire closed using a pair of pliers. Repeat the whole process to make the second earring.

Tiered Necklace

This chunky, three-tiered necklace lends itself particularly well to wooden beads, which give a very warm, tactile feel to jewellery. Wooden beads are widely available in many shapes and sizes, either carved or plain, coloured or simply with a varnished, natural-wood finish. This necklace is deceptively quick to make – the beads are simply threaded on to the three strings, which are taken through a large bead at either end and attached to a fastening. The same order of beads has been used here on each strand, with a graduation from the central bead. Experiment with the layout of your beads first to find the most attractive design before stringing them together.

~

MATERIALS AND EQUIPMENT

• assorted beads of your choice • fine bonded-nylon or button thread, close to colours of beads • scissors • fine beading needle • 2 large round beads and 2 small round beads for the ends of the necklace • bolt-ring and split-ring fastening

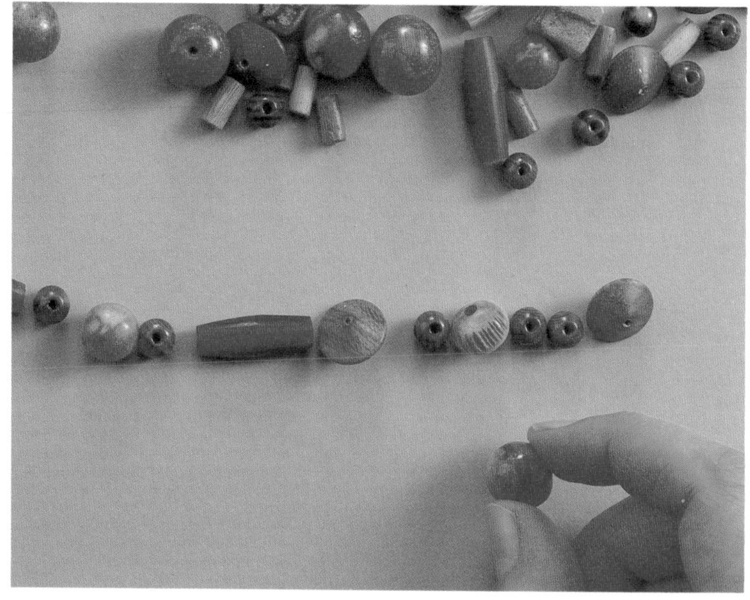

1 Arrange the beads on a cloth placed on your table or work surface, so that they will not roll about, to establish the order in which they will lie. It is a good idea to select a central bead first, and to work out each side from this.

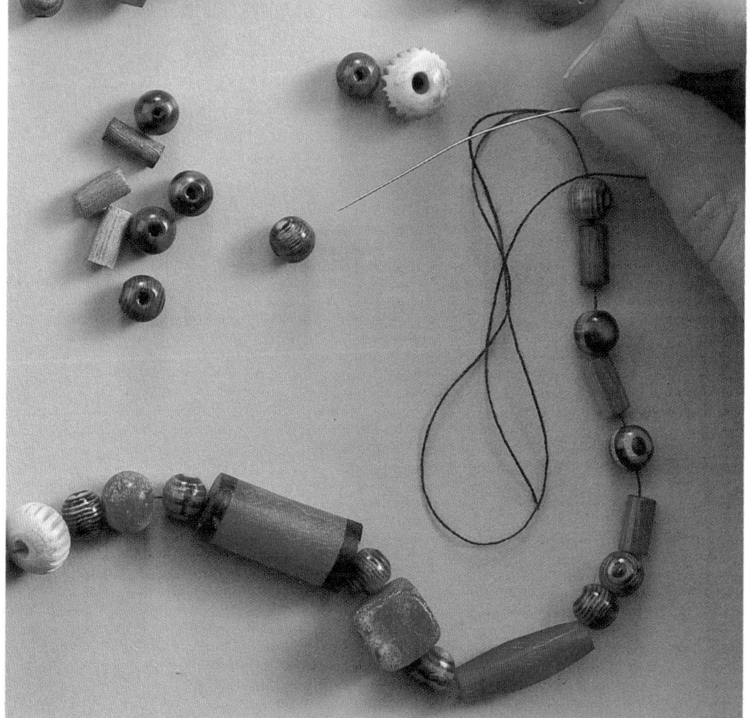

2 Decide on the length that you wish the first string of the necklace (the row that will lie nearest to your neck) to be, and take a piece of thread at least 25 cm (10 in) longer than this to allow for finishing off the string at a later stage. Thread up the needle and pick up the first row of beads, leaving the ends of the thread free at either end.

3 Pick up the remaining two rows in this way, adding 4-5 cm ($1\frac{1}{2}$ – 2 in) in length to each row, and lay them out to check the sequence and the way in which they will lie. Thread up the loose thread at one end of the necklace on to the needle, and take them through one big bead and one smaller bead to bring the three rows together. Repeat at the other end.

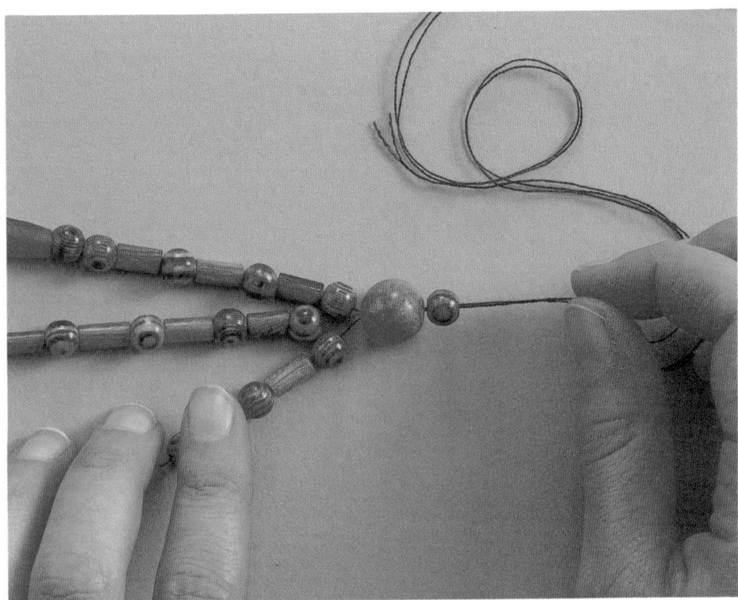

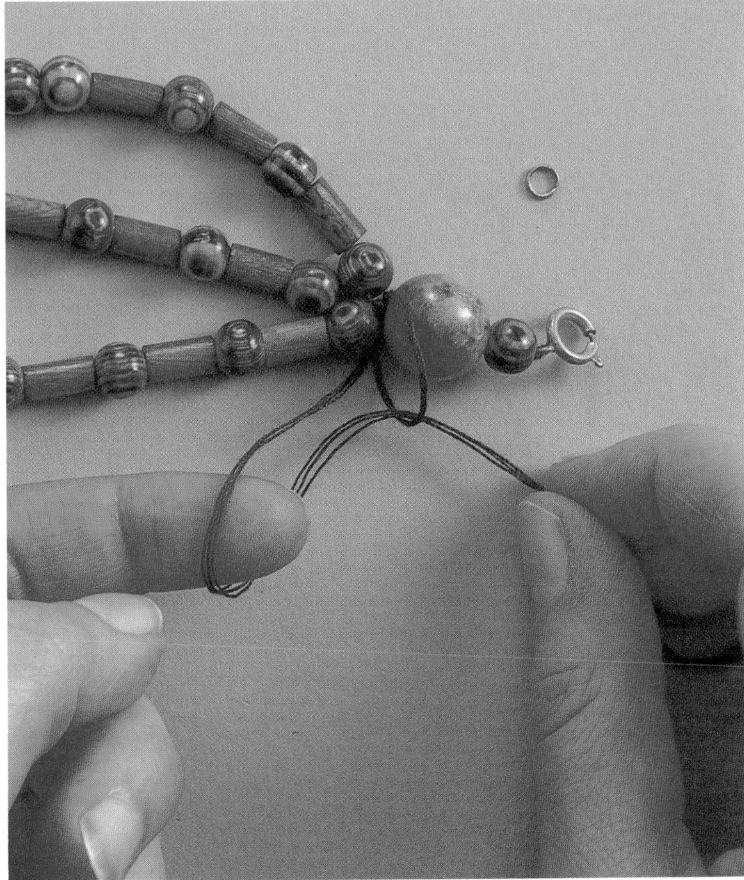

4 Work the ends around the bolt-ring fastening (threading each thread individually through the needle), and take all the ends back down through the large bead. Knot the ends around the existing thread, run them back through the three rows and snip close to the work. Repeat at the other end with the split-ring fastening.

Fruit Napkin Rings

Delicate silver napkin rings adorned with small bunches of beaded fruit look stunning on plain white table-linen. The fruits are made by covering wooden beads with strings of small rocaille beads, with rocailles also used for the stems and leaves. This project takes a little time and patience to work, but the finished results are well worth the effort. The little bunches of cherries, blueberries, blackberries and raspberries look almost good enough to eat.

~

MATERIALS AND EQUIPMENT

- *nylon-monofilament fishing line* • *scissors*
- *fine beading needle*
- *silver rocaille beads*
- *pea-sized wooden beads*
- *rocaille beads in 4 metallic 'fruit' colours*
- *green rocailles*
- *dressmaking pin*

1 To create the closely woven mesh which forms the 'base' of these napkin rings, you need to build up a strip of work, starting from a single row of 13 rocaille beads. To do this, take an open-arm's length of the fishing line, and thread up the needle. Tie on a silver rocaille (see 'Starting Beadwork' on page 18) and then pick up 12 more rocailles. Let them fall to the base of the thread, and, holding them with your left hand, and with your palm towards you, take the needle down through the third rocaille from the top (the eleventh rocaille).

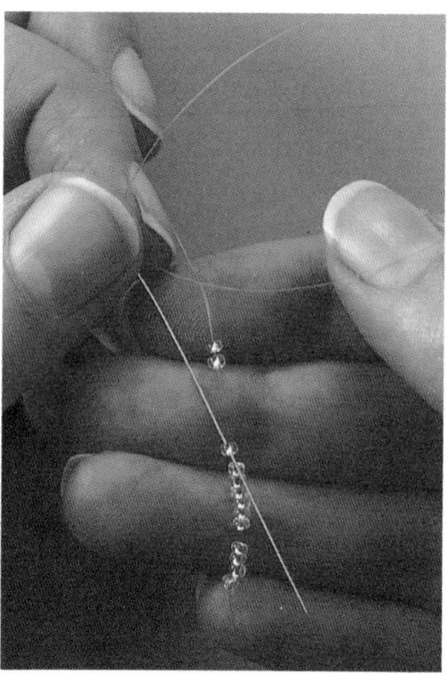

2 Repeat this process down the whole row, by picking up one rocaille and taking the needle into the next rocaille but one. There will be six rocailles in this row, and the thirteenth rocaille picked up will become the first rocaille of the second row.

3 To turn for the next row (row three), pick up one rocaille and pass it up through the last rocaille of the previous row, which will be jutting out. Then pick up the next rocaille, and pass through the next bead on the previous row, which will also be jutting out. Continue in this way to build up approximately 15 cm (6 in) of work, long enough to make a napkin ring.

To mesh the ends together, make sure that the working thread is coming out at the opposite edge to the edge at which you started. Instead of picking up a turning bead, take the thread into the top bead of the first row, back through the next jutting-out bead on the last row, and so on, until the two edges form a closed, meshed surface. Finish with a knot, and take the thread back through the work, knotting here and there to secure. Snip close to the beads.

4 To make a covered bead, take an open-arm's length of thread (this should be sufficient to cover two beads), and knot on the first rocaille (see 'Starting Beadwork' on page 18). Next, thread on the wooden bead, which is to be covered with rocailles. Leave a 'tail' of approximately 25 cm (10 in), with which to make the stalk and leaf at a later stage.

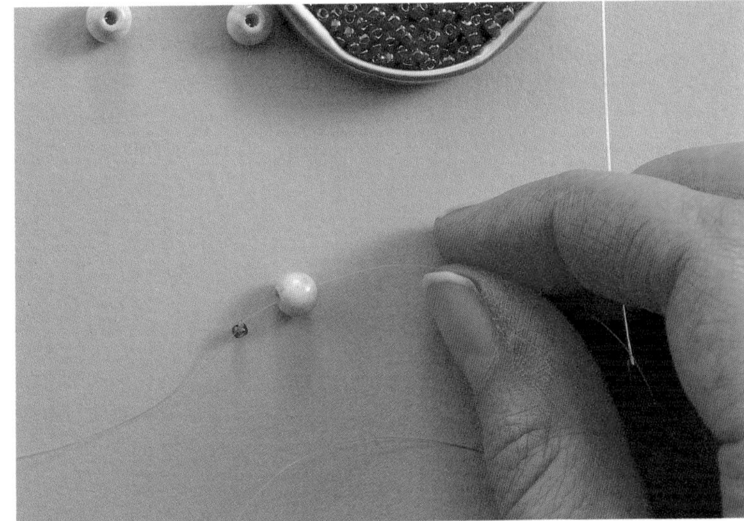

5 Pick up five or six more rocailles (depending on the size of the wooden bead), and pass the needle back up through the base bead to complete the first 'cover' row.

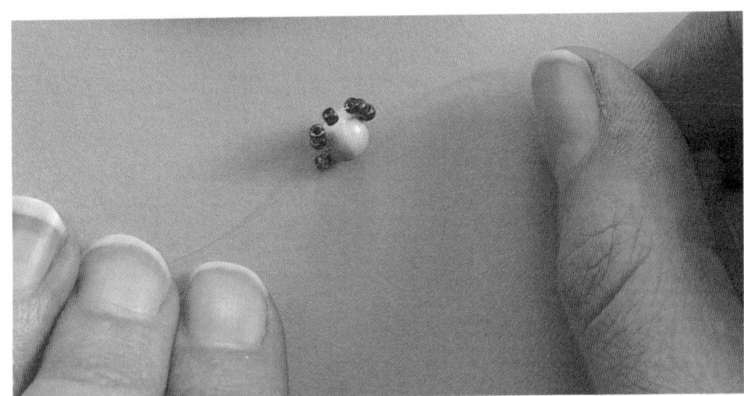

6 Repeat this process until the base bead is covered. You will find that, as the rows of rocailles cover the surface of the base bead, you will need to reduce the number of beads that you thread on in order to make the covering surface fairly even. Do not jerk the thread, as this will make the beads sit unevenly.

7 Make four of these fruit shapes. To form the stems, pick up 10 green rocailles on the first stem, and eight, six and three rocailles on the others respectively.

8 Take the last three thread ends from the shorter stems through the bottom rocaille of the longest stem.

9 Draw up the stems and make a knot with all the threads, using a pin to slide the knot down into place.

10 To make a leaf, thread up one of the ends that you have just tied. Pick up 10 green rocailles and, missing out the top bead, pass the needle down through the next bead.

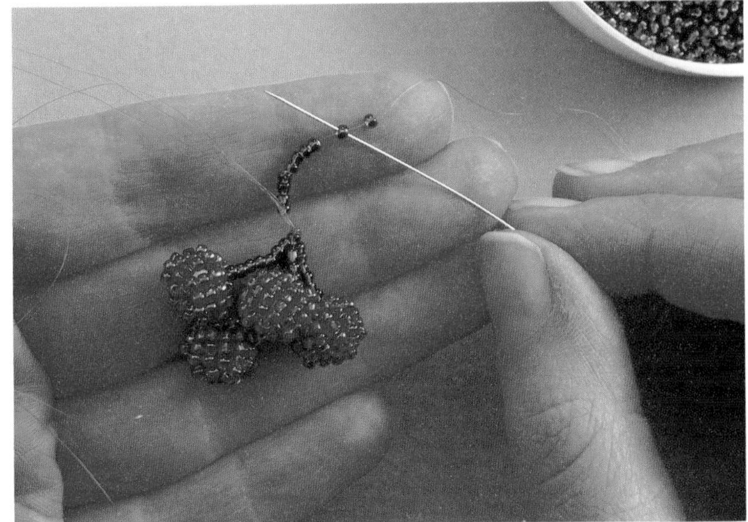

11 To complete the leaf shape, pick up eight rocailles, and pass the needle down one of the stems and into the fruit beads. Take the thread end back in through the lines of beads, knotting here and there as you go. Snip off the end close to the work.

12 Repeat the process with the other three thread ends to make three more leaf shapes. To attach the bunch of fruit to the napkin ring, take a new thread and work it a little way into the napkin-ring rocailles. Position the bunch of fruit where you would like it to sit, and work several oversewn stitches around the stems of the fruit. Knot the thread to secure, take it back through the beads and snip the end close to the work.

Tube Bracelet and Necklace

THE DELICATE, almost snake-like tube structure of this jewellery looks wonderfully ornate, but is in fact very simple to work. It is formed by building up the rows of beads in a long spiral, the ends of which are then sewn together. A looped edging in a contrasting colour, shown here on the necklace, can be added to the curved surface to provide further interest. Several tubes lying together on the neck or wrists would create a really dramatic effect.

~

MATERIALS AND EQUIPMENT

• *nylon-monofilament fishing line (1.8 kg/4 lb breaking strength)* • *scissors* • *fine beading needle* • *rocaille beads in one or two colours*

. . . . . .

1 To make the bracelet, first thread up an open-arm's length of fishing line on to the beading needle (for the necklace, you will need approximately three times this length). Tie on the first rocaille bead (see 'Starting Beadwork' on page 18), leaving an end long enough to thread a short way back into the work at a later stage. Pick up 11 more rocailles, and pass the needle back through the first one to form the base circle.

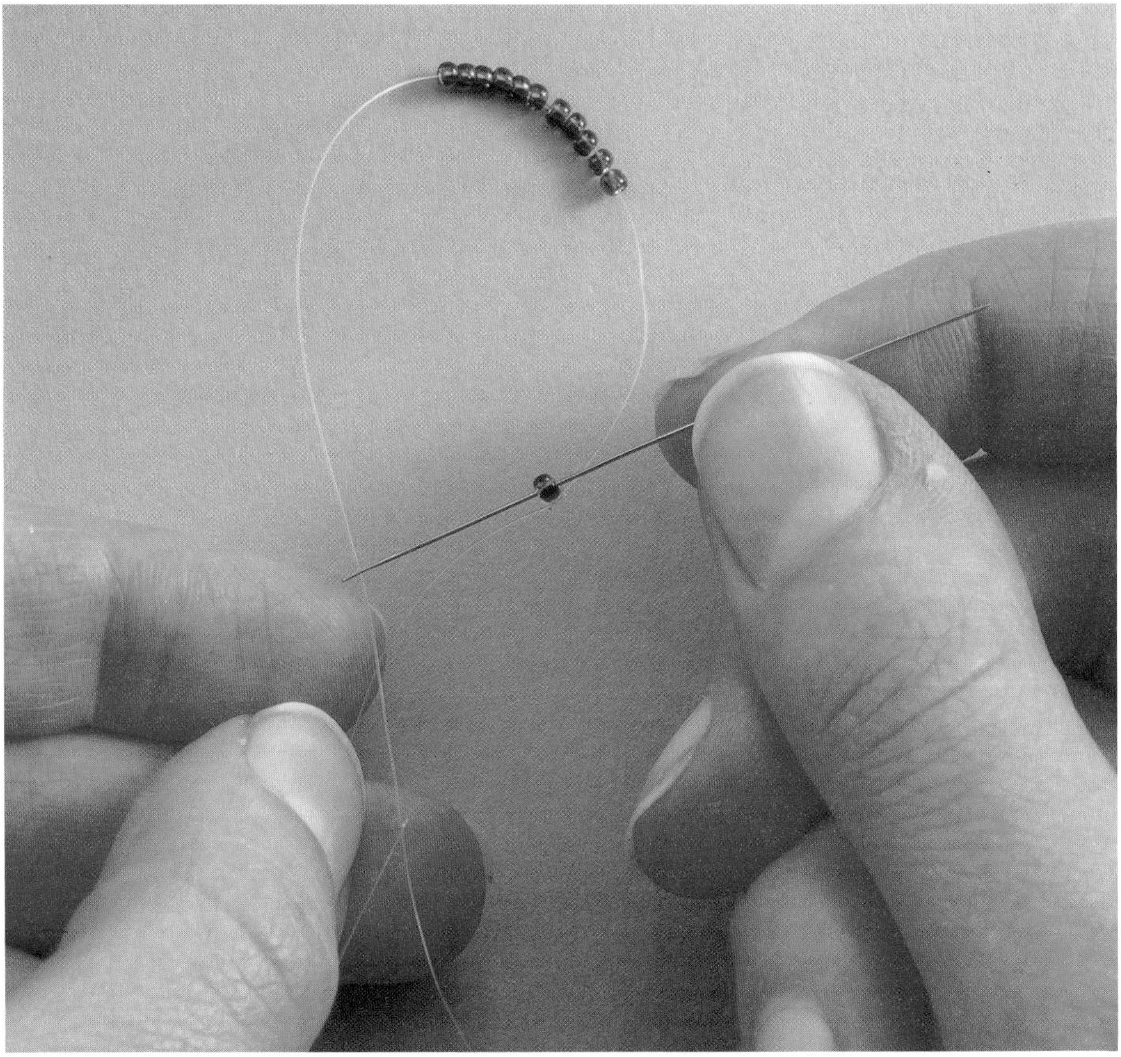

2 Pick up five more rocailles (the central rocaille can be a contrasting colour if you wish). Missing out three rocailles in the base circle, take the needle along through the fourth bead in the circle.

3 Repeat this process twice more, each time missing out three rocailles and passing through the fourth. This will bring you out at the very first rocaille that you tied on. You will have three loops at this stage.

4 To begin the next row, pick up another five rocailles (including the central contrasting colour, if used), and pass through the central rocaille of the first loop on the first row. This is important, as it is the step which takes you into the tube effect.

Pick up five more rocailles, and take the needle through the central bead of the next loop. Continue in this way, always picking up five beads, and always passing through the central bead of the next loop, until you have worked approximately 20 cm (8 in) of tube.

5 To make the end of the bracelet a little smaller, reduce the pick up from five to three beads (no contrasting colour is needed here). Do this three times in all. Tie a knot with your working thread around the thread of the work at this point, to secure the end row.

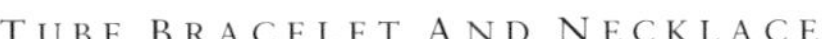

6 To join the two ends of the tube, hold the ends together in one hand. Take the needle through three rocailles on the opposite end row and back through three rocailles on the working end row to draw the edges together. Repeat this until the two ends butt together completely. Take the working thread back into the beads and snip it close. Thread up the end that you left at the beginning of the work, and take this back into the beads.

7 To form a looped edging (shown on the necklace in the finished project), take a new, small open-arm's length of thread and take it into the work, knotting here and there on the thread. Bring the thread out at one of the contrasting-coloured rocailles. Pick up eight rocailles in the contrasting colour and take the needle forward into one of the contrasting rocailles lying diagonally in front. You could work this looped edging around the whole surface or just one section of it, depending on the finished look that is required.

MOONSHOWER HAT

ANY PLAIN, pull-on hat will be transformed and given a new lease of life with the addition of bead decoration. On this hat, silver bugle beads and transparent magatama beads depicting a galaxy of moons and stars make a wonderful contrast to the black felt; V-shapes around the top edge of the hat bring all the beadwork together. On this style of hat, the decoration looks particularly effective around the brim, as well as on the crown, but the beads can, of course, be added to any part of the hat, in any quantity you wish.

~

MATERIALS AND EQUIPMENT

- *fine beading needle*
- *cotton sewing thread in colour to match hat*
- *scissors* • *plain fabric hat* • *silver bugle beads*
- *transparent magatama beads (these have an off-centre hole)*
- *tailor's chalk*

. . . . . .

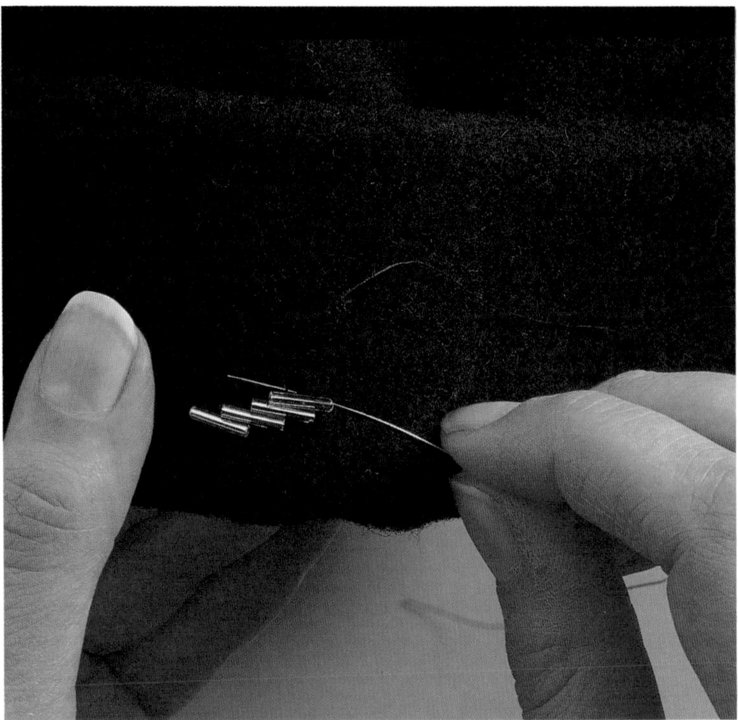

1 Thread up the needle with a single-arm's length of sewing thread, and make a knot at the end. Find the centre front of the hat, and bring the thread out to the right side, approximately 1.5 cm ($\frac{1}{2}$ in) from the bottom edge of the brim. Pick up a bugle bead on the thread, let it fall up to the hat and position it so that it lies horizontally. Take the needle into the hat at the end of the bugle, ready to sew on the next bead. Sew on four bugles in this staggered formation to create the bottom curve of the moon.

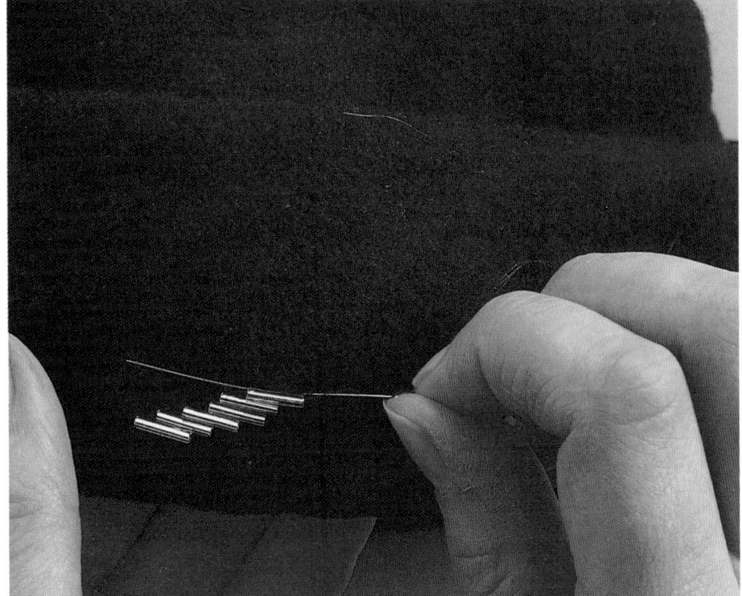

2 Build up the next phase of the moon by sewing on three more bugles, slightly less staggered than the first four beads.

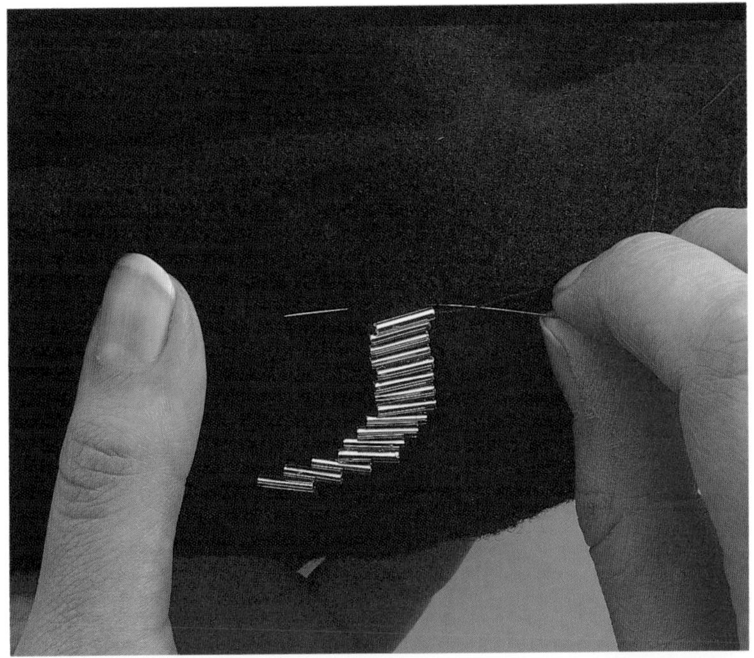

3 Create the heart of the moon by sewing on eight bugles that sit on top of one another.

4 Complete the top curve of the moon by sewing on the last five bugle beads. Stagger these beads again, as with the first beads, but this time in the opposite direction. When you have completed the moon, end off the thread neatly on the inside of the hat.

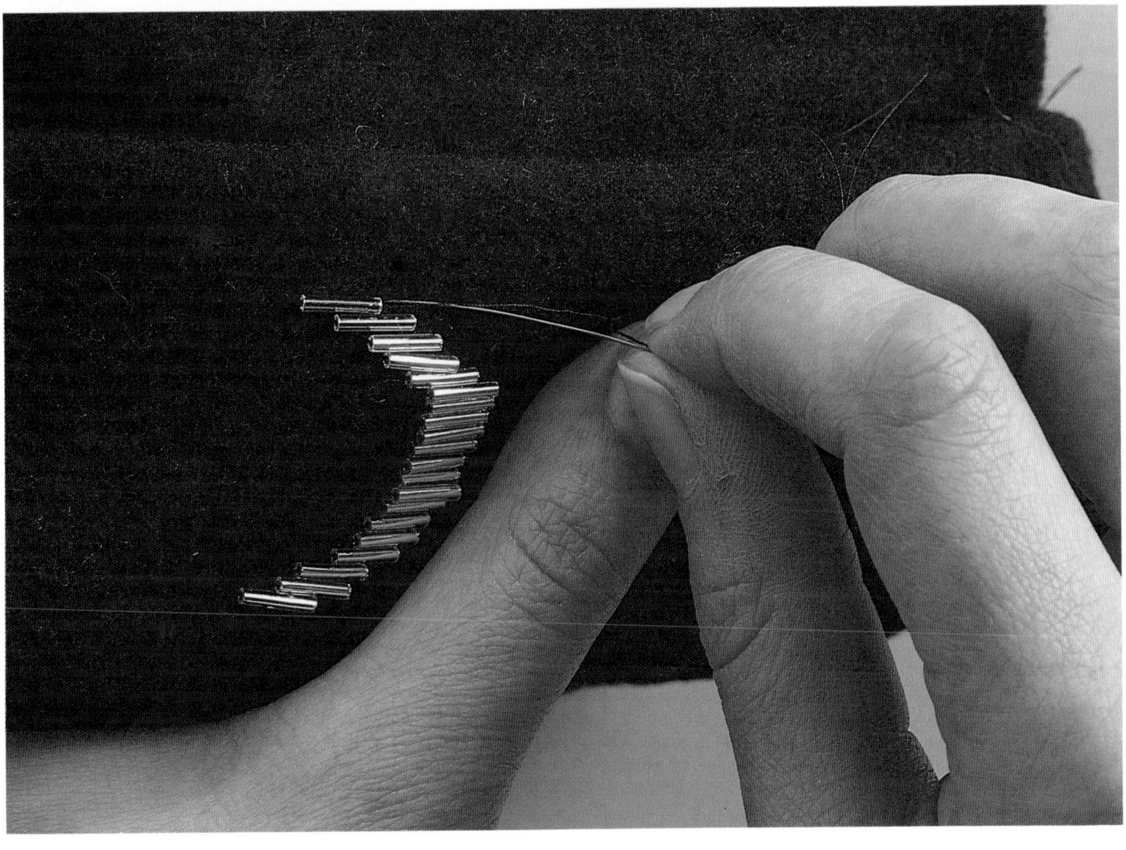

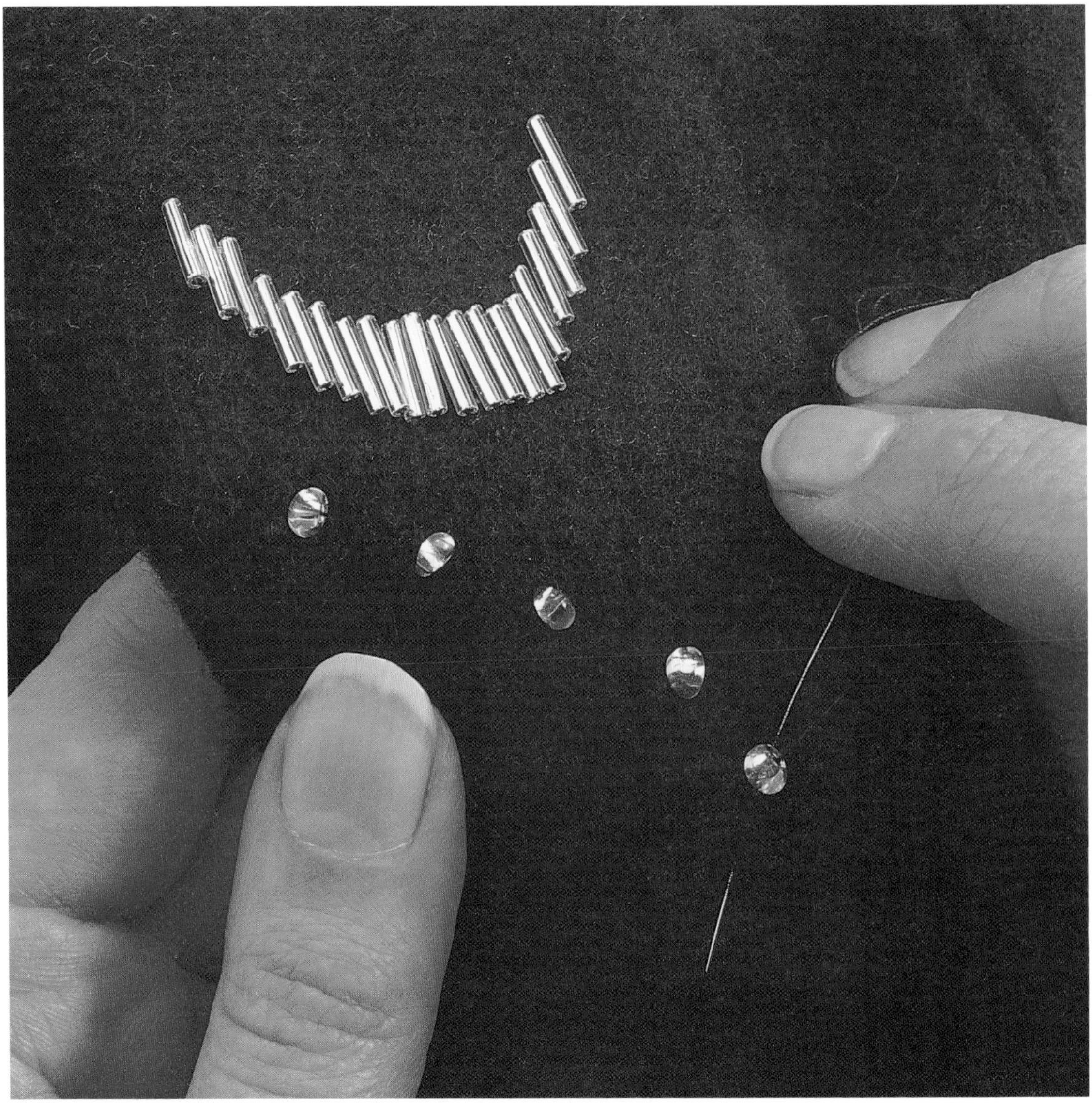

5 Repeat the moon shape wherever you wish on the hat. On this example, there are four moons spaced equally around the brim and one on the crown, all facing in the same direction. Once all the moons are in place, think about some celestial accompaniment. Take as many magatama beads as you require, and use tailor's chalk to mark the points at which you wish to position the beads. To sew on the beads, make a knot at the end of a new piece of thread, and bring the thread out at the right side of the hat. Pick up a bead and let it fall to the hat. Using a backstitch motion, take the needle into the hat, and out at the point where the next bead will lie.

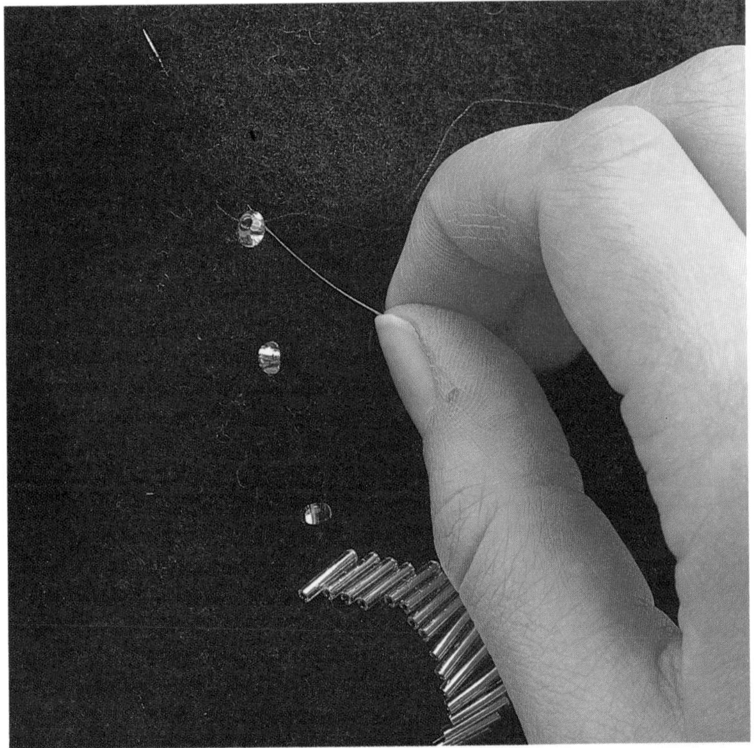

6 To work the shower of 'stars' on the crown of the hat, first sew a single line of beads starting at the top of the moon and working straight towards the centre back of the crown. Use a backstitch to sew the beads, so that the needle comes out of the fabric each time in the correct position for the next bead.

7 Look at the hat at this point, and decide whether you feel that you have decorated it enough, or whether you would like to include further decoration. The finishing touches on this example were small 'V' shapes, created with two bugles on one side of the 'V' and one on the other, positioned around the top seam on the hat, but you could of course add any other decoration of your choice.

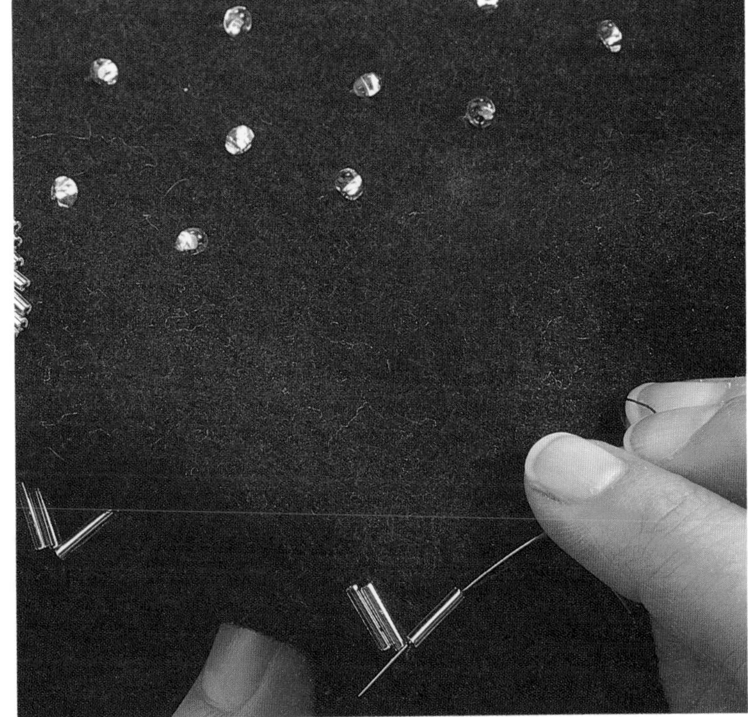

CONSTANT
QUARTZ

Woven Watchstrap

A strap made of beads woven in an attractive design turns an ordinary watch into an elegant accessory. The two-colour pattern woven here is based on a beautiful Celtic spiral design, which works very well with the oval watch face. It is a good idea to experiment with graph paper and coloured pencils before starting the weaving to find a pattern that suits your particular watch. The simple strap fastening has a wooden bead covered with rocaille beads to match the strap at one end, and a beaded loop at the other.

~

MATERIALS AND EQUIPMENT

• *watch face* • *graph paper* • *coloured pencils* • *scissors* • *fine bonded-nylon thread* • *fine beading needle* • *bead loom* • *rocaille beads in your choice of colours* • *cotton binding tape, slightly narrower than width of bars on watch* • *cotton sewing thread* • *wooden bead for covering*

. . . . . .

1 This watchstrap is made from two identical strips of beadwork which fit on either side of the watch face. To establish the length required for each strip, measure the overall length of the strap and watch. Subtract the width of the watch itself, and halve the remaining length. The width of the weaving will obviously depend on the width of the bars on the watch, to which it will be attached. Work out the pattern of the weaving on graph paper, using coloured pencils. Thread up the loom (see page 16) with the required number of warp threads and work one strip of weaving, for half of the strap.

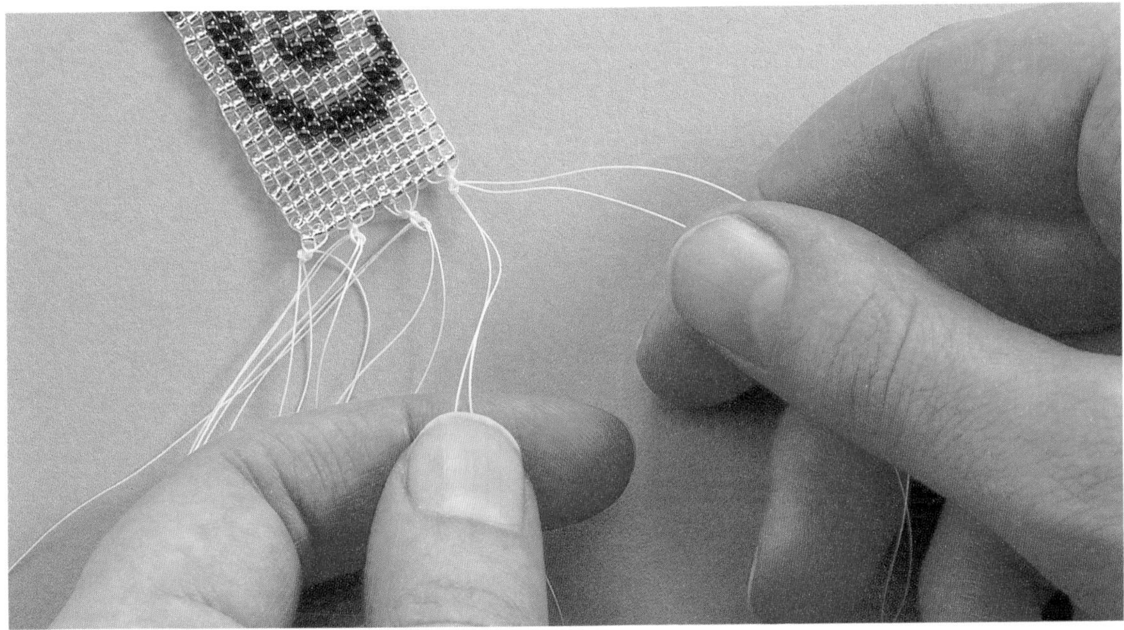

2 Carefully cut the completed strip of weaving from the loom, leaving the warp threads sufficiently long to enable you to tie them off. Tie pairs of thread ends together with double knots to secure the weaving.

3 Lay these knotted warp threads flat along the surface at each end of the weaving. Bring a new thread into the beads, securing it with a knot, and oversew the warp threads to the weaving, working the thread through several rows.

4 Cut a piece of the cotton binding tape long enough to cover the weaving, plus a small hem at one end and 5 cm (2 in) to overlap at the other end (this end will be attached to the watch face). Oversew the binding tape neatly to the back of the weaving with cotton sewing thread, catching the stitches on the edge warp threads and turning under a hem at the end.

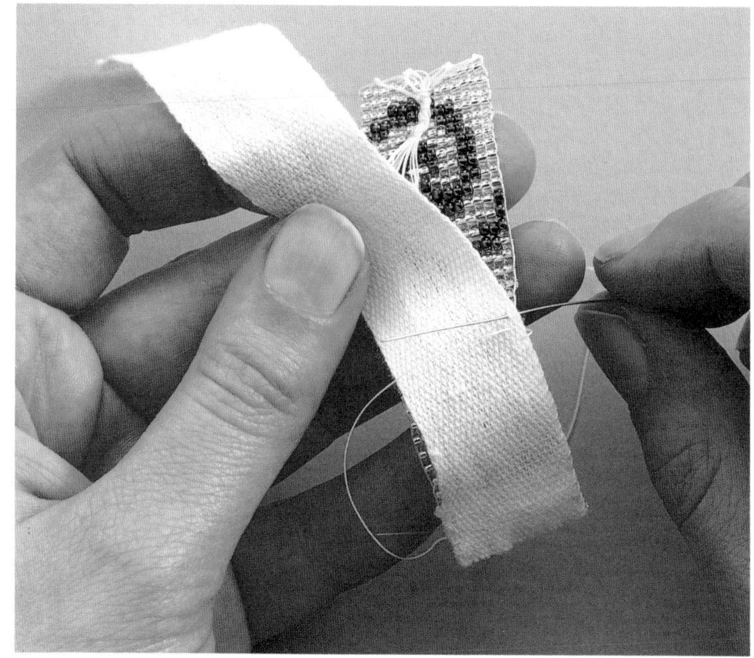

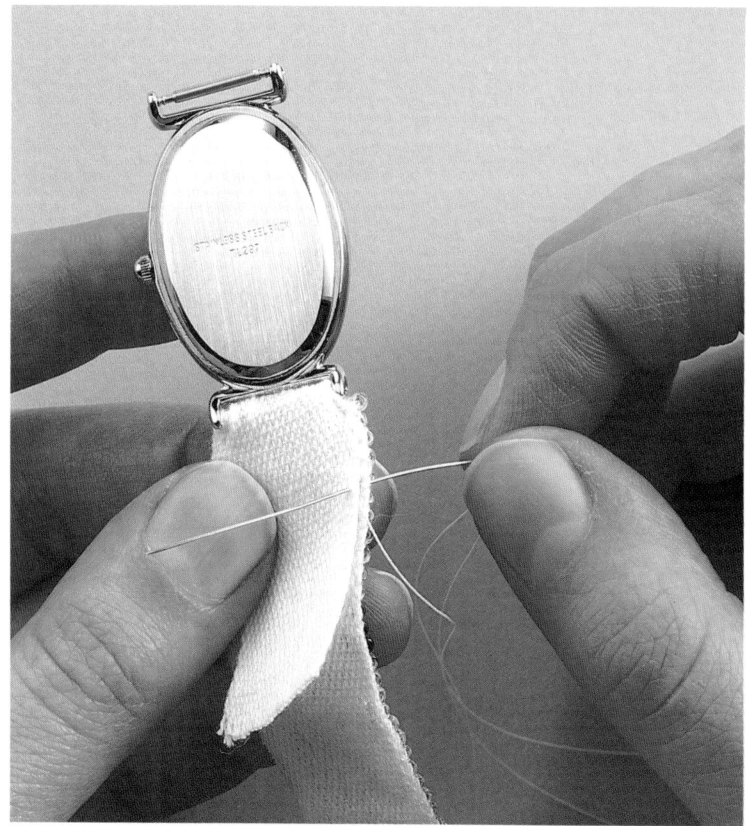

5 To attach the completed strap to the watch face, thread the unbeaded piece of tape through the bar on one side of the watch. Fold over the tape and oversew the edges to the back of the strap. Knot the thread end securely.

6 Repeat the whole process to make the second half of the strap. Make a covered fastening bead and attach it to one end of the strap, following the instructions given on pages 20–21. (The fastening shown here uses three strands of the design colour, as well as the main colour of beads, to co-ordinate with the strap itself.)

7 Make a beaded-loop fastening for the opposite end of the strap, following the instructions on pages 22–23.

ALLIGATOR EARRINGS

THE DETAIL of these delightful earrings makes them look remarkably realistic. They are made entirely of small rocaille beads – green for the alligator's back, silver for the belly and black for the feet. The beading is worked using two beading needles and a single thread, and the finished earrings are suspended from simple ear-wires attached to the alligator's 'tail'. They are very quick to make, and would make wonderful little presents for Christmas or a birthday.

~

MATERIALS AND EQUIPMENT

• nylon-monofilament fishing line (note: black thread has been used here for clarity) • scissors • 2 fine beading needles • small green, silver and black rocaille beads • 2 earring wires • pliers

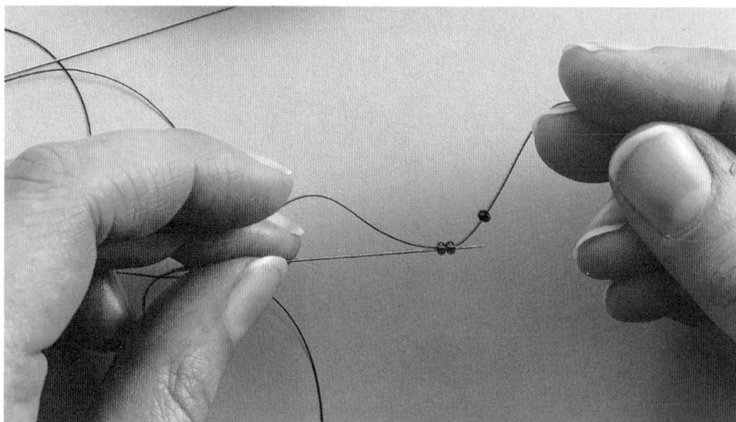

1 Take approximately 1 metre (1¼ yards) of fishing line, and thread on a needle at either end. With the right-hand needle, pick up two green and one black rocaille beads and allow them to fall to the middle of the thread.

2 Take the left-hand needle and pass it back through the two green rocailles only.

3 Pull up the thread so that the beads lie close together, forming a small triangle. Next, pick up two silver rocailles on the left-hand needle, pass the right-hand needle back through them, and pull closed. The silver rocailles will now lie beneath the green.

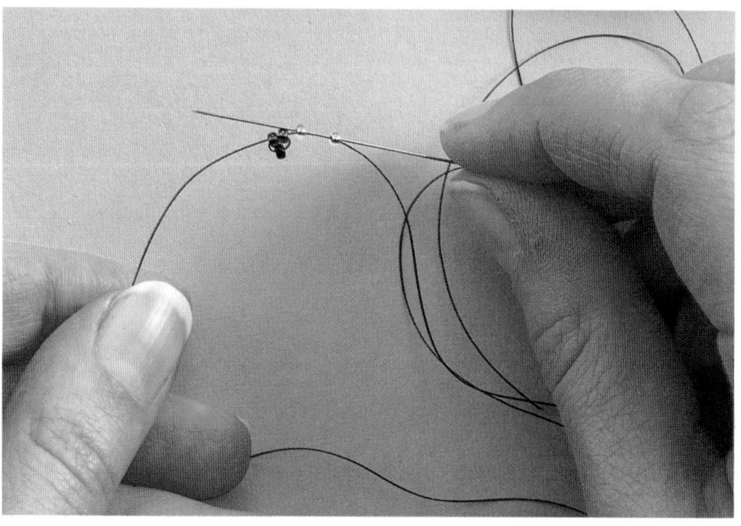

4 Increase to three green and four silver rocailles, then work a row of four green rocailles and the matching row beneath of four silver rocailles. (Note: with every top green row, a matching silver row is threaded, to form the under-part of the alligator.) When you reach the fifth row you can thread in the eyes, so pick up one green, one black, one green, one black and one green rocaille, and complete this row. Then thread on the fifth row of silver rocailles.

5 To shape the head of the alligator, on the sixth row decrease to four green rocailles and four silver rocailles. The front legs are formed on the seventh row (the neck row). To make these legs, use the left-hand needle to thread on three green rocailles in the usual way, to form the top half of the neck. On the right-hand needle, pick up three green and four black rocailles and take the needle back down through the three green (leg) rocailles. This forms a tiny foot at the end of the leg.

6 Do the same on the left-hand side, so that the threads come out on each side of the neck. To complete the neck row underneath, pick up three silver rocailles on the left-hand needle and let them fall to the end of the thread. Pass the right-hand needle through the silver rocailles.

7 To build up the alligator's body, work one row with four rocailles (first green, and then silver) top and bottom, one row with five rocailles top and bottom, and three rows with six rocailles top and bottom. Decrease to five rocailles top and bottom, then down to four, and then thread on the three top tail row rocailles, where the back legs are formed. Complete these in the same way as the front legs. To vary the feet slightly, pass the needle back into the first black rocaille to create a different end. Thread on the silver row underneath.

8 To form the alligator's tail, decrease by working two rows of two rocailles (first green, and then silver) top and bottom, and then one row of one rocaille. Tie the two working-thread ends in a knot.

9 To make the loop from which to hang the alligator, pick up six green rocailles on either the right or left-hand needle, and take the same needle round through the beads, including the tail-tip bead. Work this thread end back into the body, knotting here and there on the thread as you go. Snip the thread close to the beads, and repeat with the other thread end.

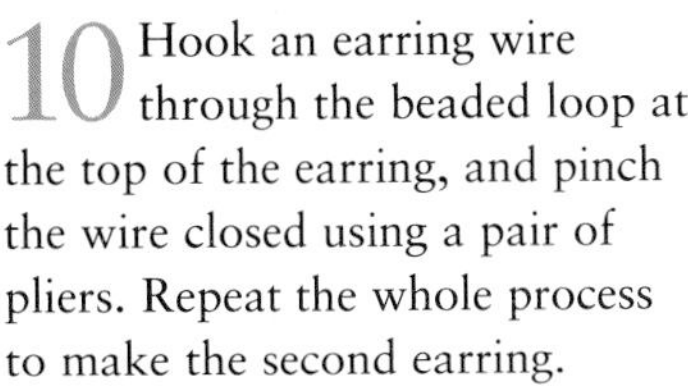

10 Hook an earring wire through the beaded loop at the top of the earring, and pinch the wire closed using a pair of pliers. Repeat the whole process to make the second earring.

Hair Ornaments

Beads lend themselves beautifully to hair ornaments. This beaded design has been threaded on to cotton-covered shirring elastic, making it flexible enough to be used over a pony tail or slipped on to a hair comb, as well as sewn on to a fabric hair clip, as shown here.

The decoration is made from a base circle of transparent magatama beads, from which three rows of overlapping loops are worked. The loops incorporate disc-shaped wooden beads, with three larger striped beads projecting from the central decoration.

~

MATERIALS AND EQUIPMENT

- *cotton-covered shirring elastic* • *scissors* • *fine sewing needle with fairly large eye* • *cotton sewing thread* • *transparent magatama beads* • *disc-shaped black wooden beads* • *striped, oval-shaped plastic beads*
- *fabric-covered hair clip*

. . . . . .

1 Take a piece of shirring elastic approximately 75 cm (30 in) long. To thread the elastic through the eye of the needle, take a short piece of cotton thread, double it up and pass the loop through the needle. Unravel some of the cotton threads covering the shirring elastic. Place the unravelled ends into the loop of cotton thread and pull the elastic through. Leave a tail of approximately 15 cm (6 in).

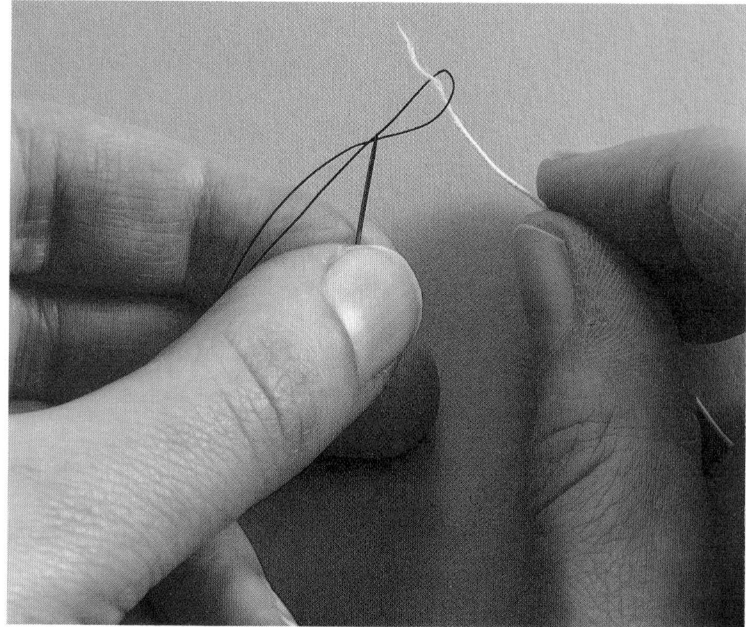

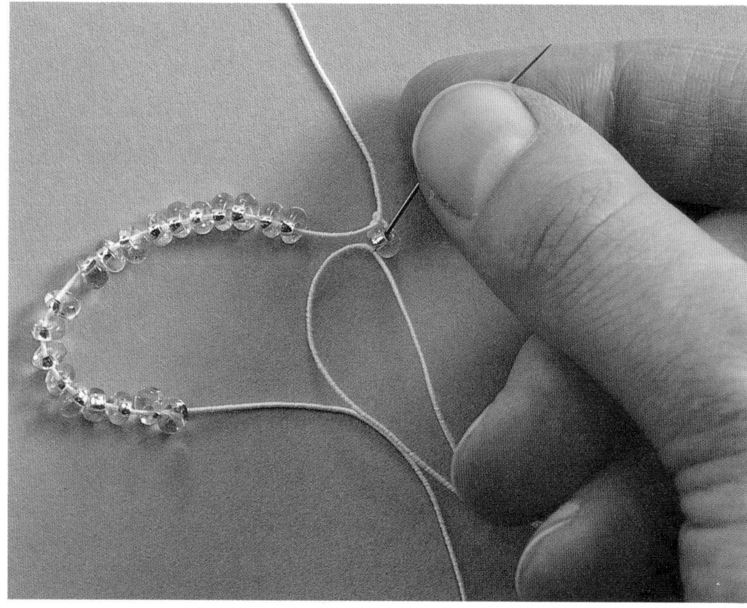

2 Tie on the first magatama bead (see 'Starting Beadwork' on page 18). Pick up 19 more beads, let them fall down the thread and then take the needle back through the first bead to form the base circle.

3 To form the first loop, pick up in turn one magatama bead, one disc-shaped bead, one large striped bead, one more disc-shaped bead and one magatama bead. Take the needle around the final magatama bead and back through the next three beads, missing out the first magatama bead, which will form the tip edge of the loop.

4 Pick up another magatama bead on the thread and, to draw this first loop closed, take the needle into the next bead but one along the base row.

5 For the second loop, thread on three magatama beads, one disc-shaped bead and three magatama beads. Missing out the first three beads on the base row, take the needle into the fourth bead.

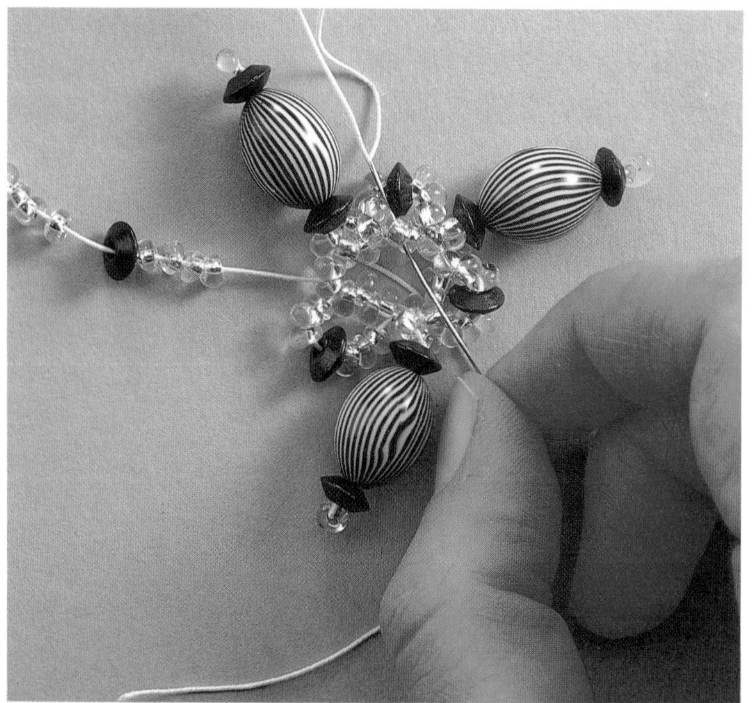

6 Complete this first row of loops, and you will find that your needle comes out virtually at the beginning, ready to work the next series of loops, which will be slightly different (there are six loops in the first row, and three loops in both the second and third rows). To form the second row, pick up four magatama beads, one disc-shaped bead and four more magatama beads. Missing out five beads on the base circle, take the needle into the sixth bead. Do this three times in all.

7 To form the final series of loops (the third row), pick up seven magatama beads and, missing the first five beads on the base circle, take the needle into the sixth bead. Do this three times in all.

8 Take the working thread back into the loops, knotting here and there on the thread in the loops to provide a secure finish. Snip the thread close to the work. Thread up the short 'tail' that was left at the beginning on to the needle, and thread this back into the work. Sew the ornament on to a fabric-covered hair clip using a doubled length of sewing thread in the needle, or, alternatively, simply slip it on to hold a pony tail in place.

Jester Collar and Bracelet

The little points on this delicate collar and bracelet are reminiscent of the bells on a jester's cap. The simple design consists of linked diamond shapes, each of which sits in a curve, and is made entirely of small rocaille beads. The collar and bracelet can be dressed up or down, depending on your mood and the occasion, and work equally well with more casual daywear or an elegant evening outfit. As well as being used for jewellery, the beadwork can also be sewn around the neckline or cuff edges to enliven a plain shirt or sweater.

~

MATERIALS AND EQUIPMENT

- *nylon-monofilament fishing line (note: black thread has been used here for clarity)* • *scissors*
- *fine beading needle*
- *small blue and black rocailles (or colours of your choice)* • *bolt-ring and split-ring fastening*

. . . . . .

1 Take an open-arm's length of the fishing line and thread up the needle. Tie on a blue rocaille bead (see 'Starting Beadwork' on page 18), leaving a 'tail' of approximately 30 cm (12 in) with which to attach the fastening at a later stage. Pick up in turn four more blue, one black, five blue, one black, seven blue and four black rocailles. Pass the needle back up through the first black rocailles of the last four that you threaded on, to form a floret-style tip.

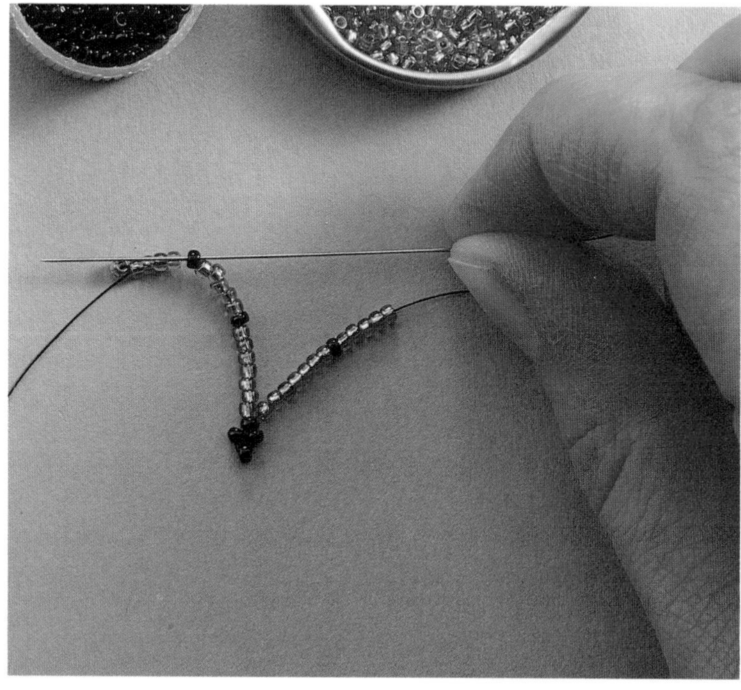

2 Pick up seven blue, one black and five blue rocailles and then take the needle up through the very first black rocaille that you threaded on. This completes the first diamond shape.

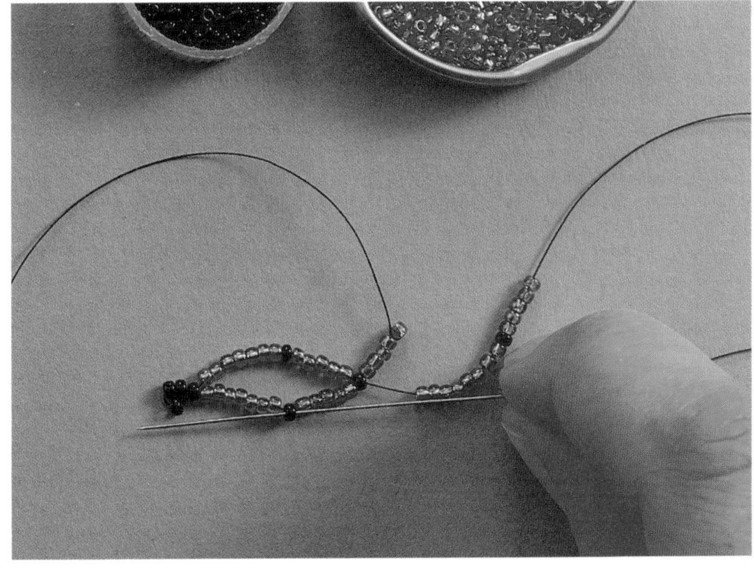

3 To form the top curve, pick up eight blue, one black and five blue rocailles. Take the needle down through the right-hand side black bead of the first diamond shape.

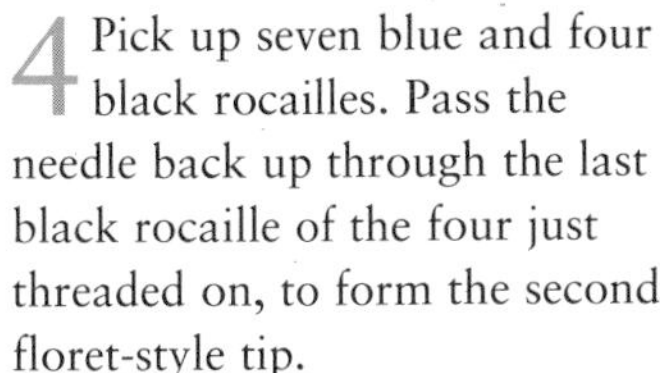

4 Pick up seven blue and four black rocailles. Pass the needle back up through the last black rocaille of the four just threaded on, to form the second floret-style tip.

5 Continue in this manner until the collar or bracelet is the required length. End off the beadwork by threading on five blue rocailles. Attach the bolt-ring fastening (see page 22) to the last of these five rocailles by oversewing securely with the working thread. Take the thread end back into the beads and snip close to the work. Use the 'tail' left at the beginning of the beading to attach the split-ring fastening in the same way.

Victorian Jug Cover

Pretty covers like this one, with beads used to weigh down the edges, were first introduced in Victorian times to protect food and drink from insects at outdoor picnics and tea-parties. They have become very popular again in recent years, and add a lovely decorative touch to an outdoor table, as well as serving a practical purpose. Brightly coloured resin beads and larger disc-shaped beads have been used here to add a modern touch to this traditional item. Small beads have also been dotted over the top to complete the cover.

~

MATERIALS AND EQUIPMENT

• *tape measure* • *jug* • *pencil* • *pair of compasses* • *dressmaking net* • *scissors* • *cotton sewing thread* • *fine beading needle* • *small, brightly coloured resin beads* • *larger disc-shaped beads* • *marker pen* • *paper*

1 Measure the diameter of the top of your jug, and add approximately 5 cm (2 in) to this diameter. Using a pencil and pair of compasses, draw a circle of this size on the net, and cut it out.

Roll up the edge of the net and sew a neat hem all the way round, using running stitch in the cotton sewing thread. This will reduce the diameter of the circle by approximately 1.5 cm (½ in).

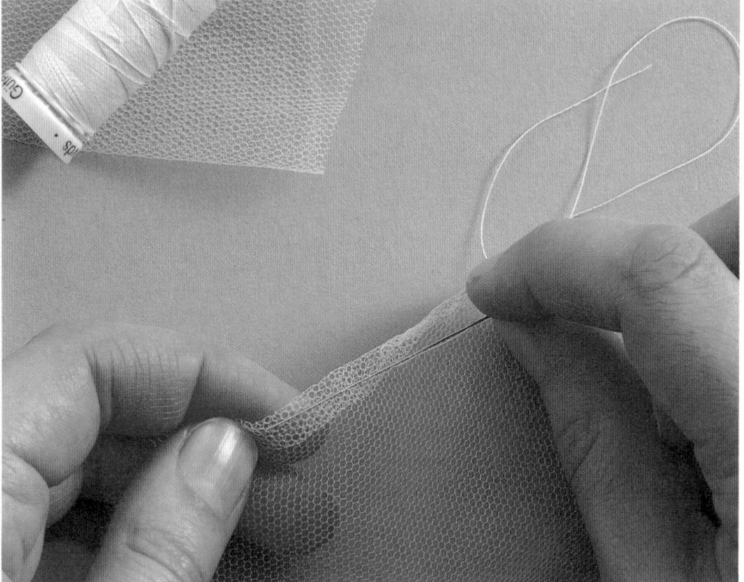

2 Attach a new thread to the edge of the net (this can be doubled if you wish). Avoid knots when attaching the thread – one or two oversewn stitches will be sufficient. (When sewing on heavier beads, and a knot is required, try to make this sit on the wrong side of the net so that it will not be visible.) Pick up the first few small beads, in your chosen sequence, followed by a disc-shaped bead and another small bead, to form the first half of a loop. Take the thread around the bottom bead, back up through the disc-shaped bead, and then thread on a few more small beads to complete the loop.

Take the needle into the edge of the net, bringing it out on the right side. Oversew one or two stitches so that the thread does not slip, and then form a larger loop, this time using two small beads and one disc-shaped bead to form the drop-edged loop.

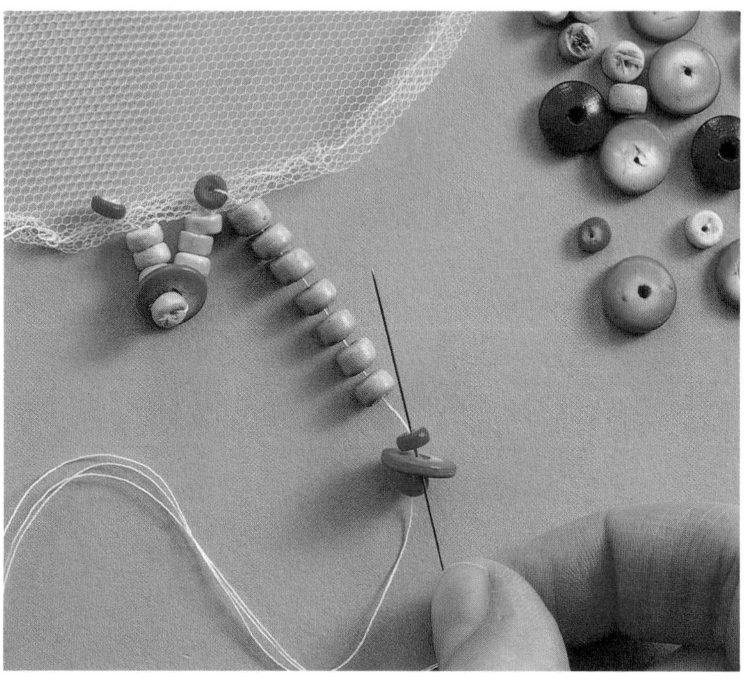

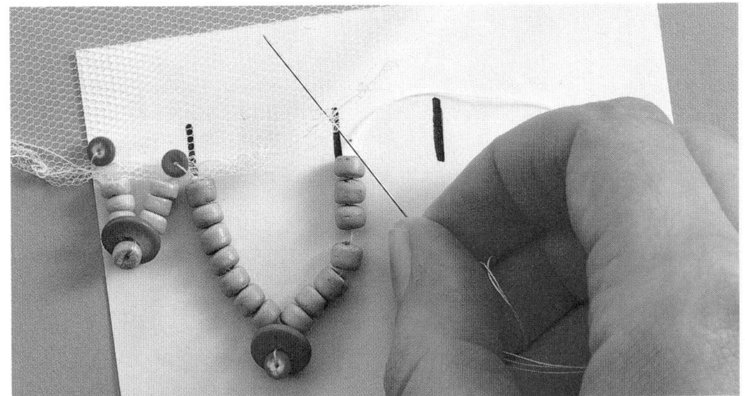

3 For the 20 cm (8 in) diameter circle shown here, 3 cm ($1\frac{1}{4}$ in) and 2 cm ($\frac{3}{4}$ in) space indicators have been marked on a piece of paper for easy measuring. Do the same for your circle, increasing or decreasing the space markers as necessary.

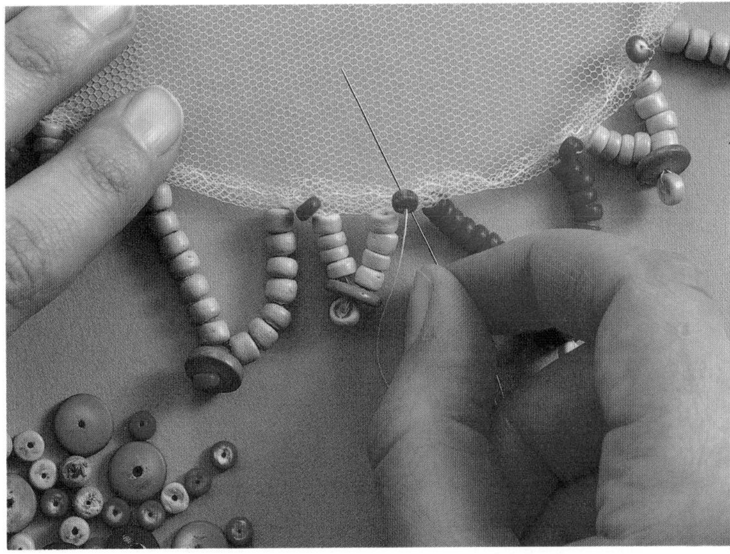

4 Working in your chosen colour sequence, continue to sew drop-edged loops all the way around the net circle. Add a bright 'spot' bead between each loop if you wish. Take your working thread back through the edge of the jug cover, securing beads here and there as you go.

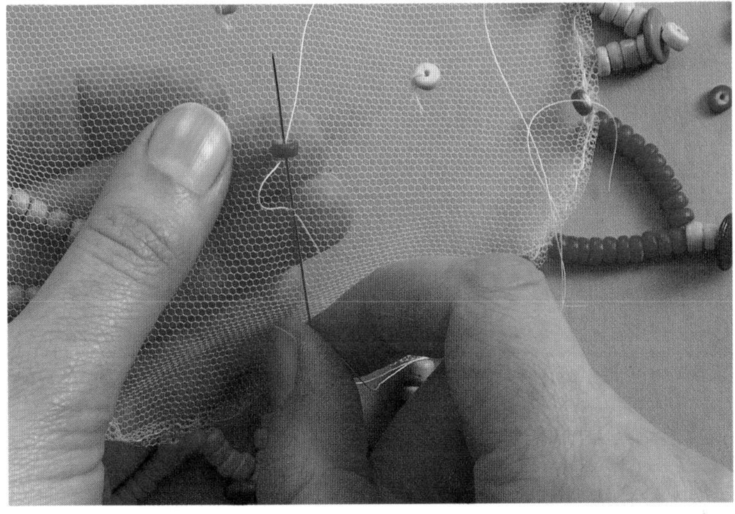

5 You can also sew on 'spot' beads as extra decoration in the middle of the net, and tie on odd beads, winding the thread through twice and tying securing knots on the wrong side of the cover. Snip off the thread ends neatly, close to the net.

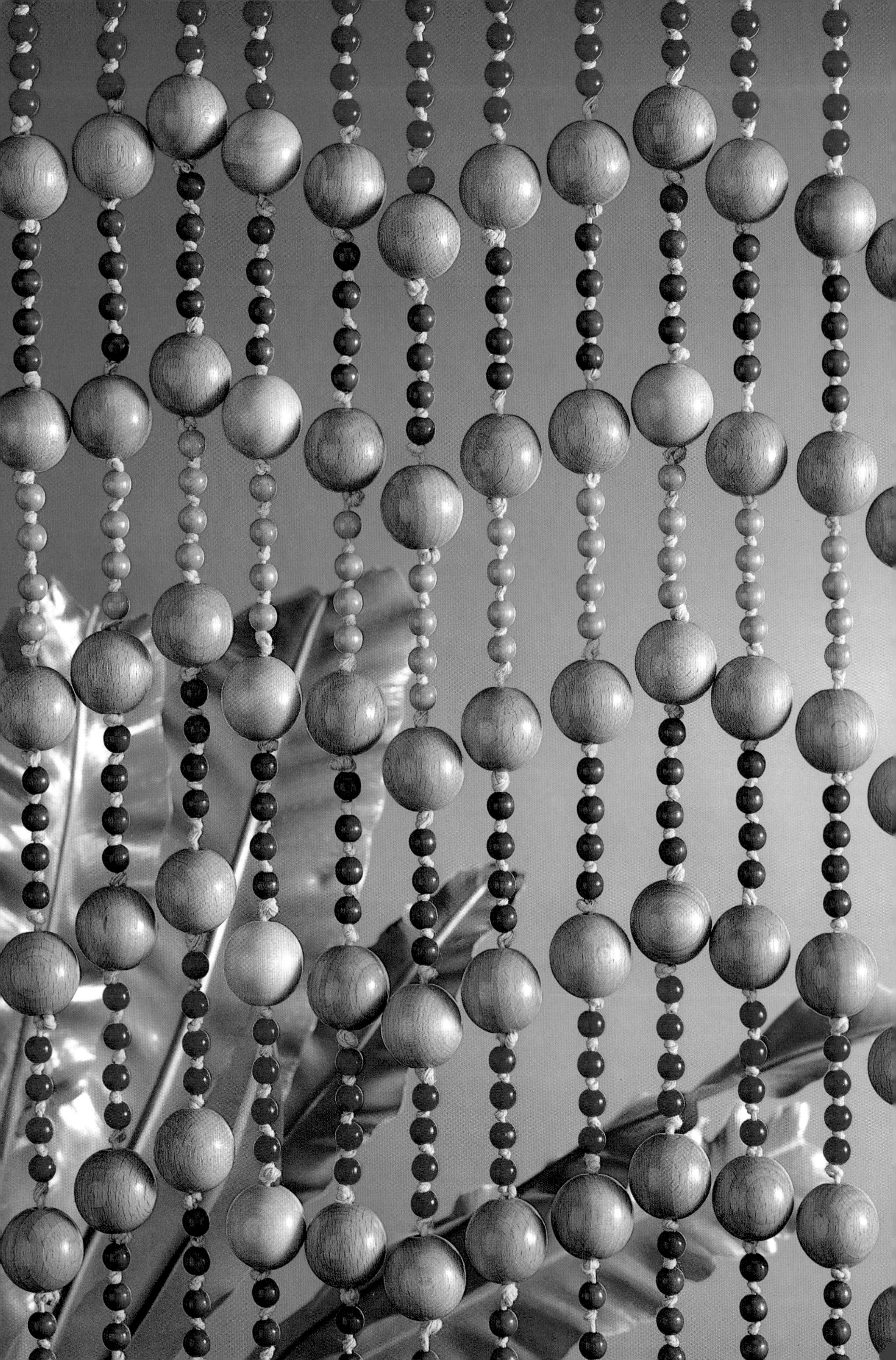

BEADED CURTAIN

A CURTAIN of colourful beads makes a beautiful feature of an uninteresting doorway or window. Wooden beads have a wonderful warm and tactile effect, and make soothing sounds as they are pushed aside or simply sway in the breeze. If the curtain is for a doorway, you will need to use fairly sturdy beads which will not shatter or chip as you walk to and fro. Household string is used as the 'thread' for this project. Here it has been used plain, in combination with brightly coloured and natural-wood beads, but you could dye the string first to produce an even more vibrant effect.

~

MATERIALS AND EQUIPMENT

• household string • scissors • paperclip or short length of wire • pliers • red, green, yellow and blue wooden beads (or colours of your choice) • natural-coloured large wooden beads • wooden dowelling • small hand saw • wood screws

1 Take a piece of string measuring twice the length of the doorway or window in which the curtain is to hang, plus approximately 75 cm (30 in). Tie one end of the string in a small loop, which will go around the wooden dowelling from which the curtain will hang.

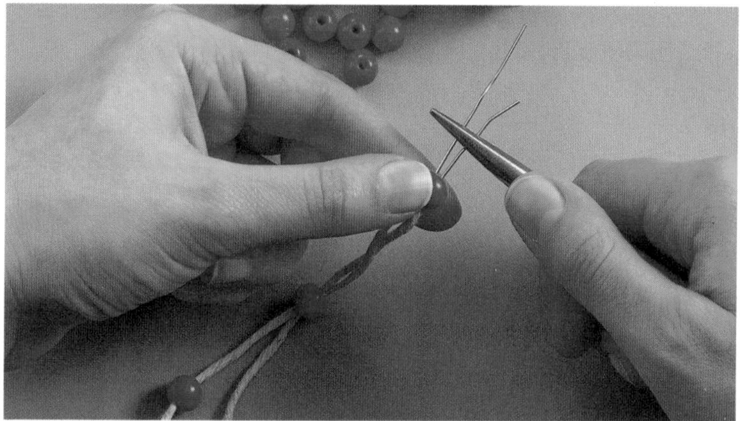

2 Straighten out the paperclip, using the pliers, and then bend it in half to make a 'V' shape. If you are using a piece of wire, simply bend it in half. Hook one end of the string into the 'V' of the paperclip or wire, and then thread on the first three red beads. Use the pliers to pull the string through the beads.

3 Push the first bead up to the loop at the end of the string. Form a knot between each bead, pushing each knot tightly up against the previous bead on the string. Make a double knot after the third bead (this knot will sit next to a large bead, so the extra bulk is necessary to prevent the larger hole from slipping over the knot).

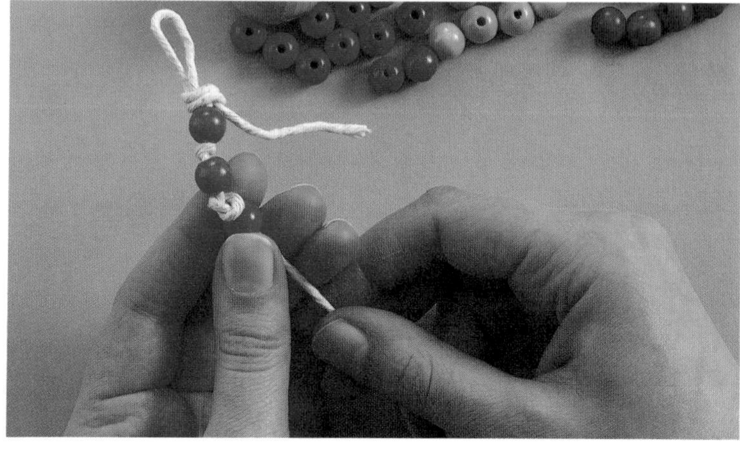

4 Thread on a large bead, and make another double knot. Thread on green beads, and another large bead, then yellow beads, and so on, until the beaded string is the correct length. To create a chevron effect in your beaded curtain, as in the example shown here, graduate the number of red beads that you thread on to the very top of each strand. This curtain started with three red beads at the top of the first strand, increased to four beads for the second row, five for the third row and six for the fourth row, then decreased back to three again, and so on. This created the chevron pattern. Four beads of each colour were worked between all the other large beads on the strands.

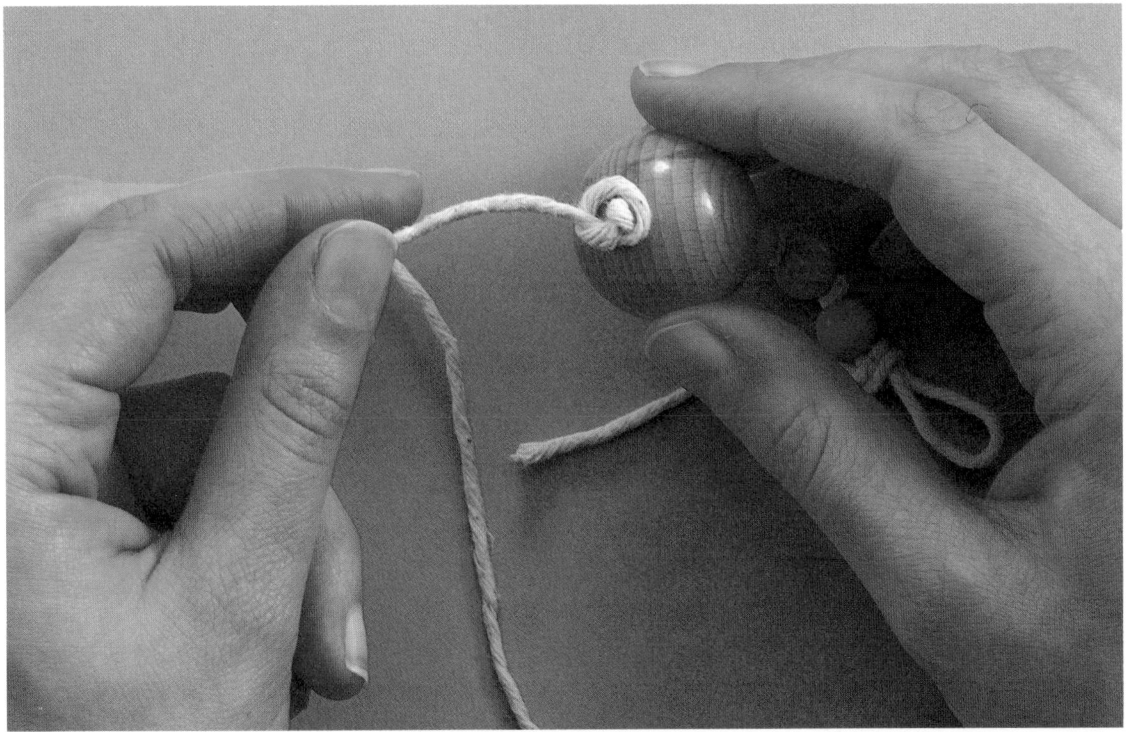

5 When you have completed the first strand of the curtain, fringe the end of the string by separating out the threads using the paperclip or wire. Continue building up the strands until you have enough lengths of knotted beads to cover your doorway or window. Make small grooves at equal intervals in the wooden dowelling, using a small hand-saw. Pass the dowelling through the loop at the top of each beaded string, and fit each string into a groove. Screw the dowelling securely into position.

Woven Bag Panels

Plain fabric bags make ideal surfaces for decoration with bright panels of woven beads, and adding beads in this way will turn a rather unexciting bag into a highly original accessory. Use coloured pencils on graph paper to create the pattern before starting the weaving, and decide on the positions of the panels, bearing in mind the use that the bag will undergo.

Additional decoration in the form of cowrie shells (often used in ethnic embroideries), more beads or unusual buttons will further enhance the woven panels. The panels are woven on a bead loom before being sewn securely to the bag.

~

MATERIALS AND EQUIPMENT

• graph paper • coloured pencils • plain fabric bag • fine bonded-nylon thread • scissors • bead loom • medium-sized rocaille beads in colours of your choice • long dressmaking pins • fine beading needle • cotton sewing thread to match colour of bag • cowrie shells (optional)

1 Work out the pattern of the panels on graph paper, using coloured pencils, taking into account how wide you wish the panels to be, as well as their positions on the bag. You might consider placing them on the straps, for example, as well as on the main body of the bag. A Native American design was used for the woven panels in this example. Thread up the loom (see page 16), and weave as many strips of beadwork as required.

2 When you have woven enough strips, cut the threads of each panel close to the knot, tying off the threads at each end as you go. Remove the work from the loom. Tie the ends of the threads in pairs, and make two knots.

3 Lay these thread ends flat against the beadwork. Work a new thread into the rows a short way, and use this to oversew the tied ends to secure them.

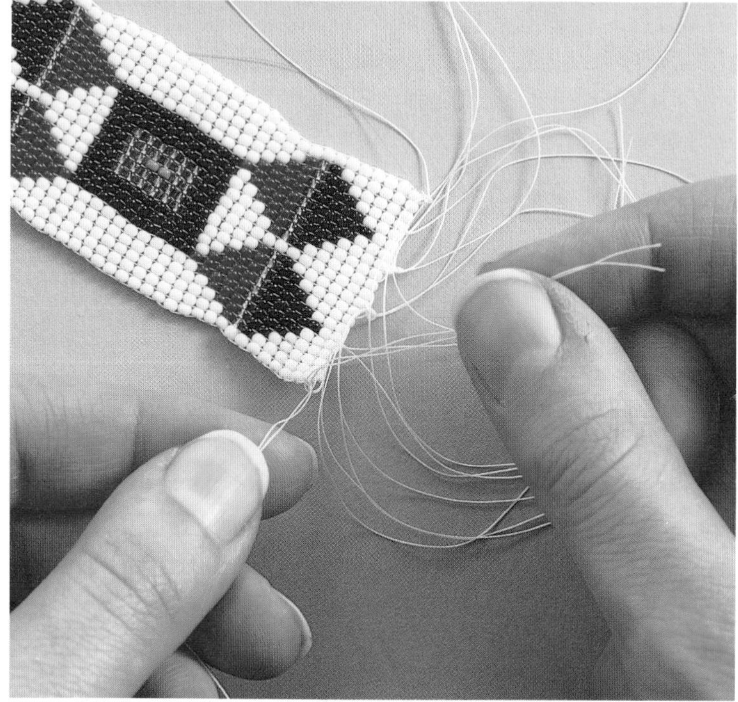

4 Position the loomed strips on the bag, and hold them in place with long dressmaking pins. Using the beading needle and sewing thread, oversew the woven panels securely. Be sure to hide any knots on the wrong side of the work.

5 If you wish to add further decoration to your bag, select unusual cowrie shells, with holes already drilled, to feature as an edging or as gap fillers. Bear in mind, however, that it is not a good idea to sew these shells on to the straps, as they may come loose – the top and sides of the bag are the best places.

Suppliers and Other Resources

Many malls offer bead stalls or stores and you will find bead stores listed in most yellow pages.

THE BEAD DIRECTORY, P.O. Box 10103, Oakland, CA 94610. A resource guide to over 400 bead stores, classes, and bead societies throughout the U.S. and Canada; cost for the third edition, $18.95 plus $3.00 shipping and handling.

BEADER'S PARADISE, P.O. Box 362, Blackfoot, ID 83221. Telephone: (208) 785-9967; 785-1838. Long time bead supplier specializing in old beads and very small beads (down to #24). Catalogue $1 upon request. Wilma Mangum.

SHIPWRECK BEADS, 2727 Westmoor Court, Olympia, WA 98502. Telephone: (206) 754-2323. Wide selection of glass beads (authorized importer of Czechoslovakian glass), stones, findings, plastic, wood, and pewter. Catalogue $4 upon request; attention: Douglas Boling.

BEAD RESEARCH ORGANIZATIONS

THE BEAD MUSEUM, 138-140 S. Montezuma, Prescott, AZ 86303. Telephone: (602) 445-2431. Director: Gabrielle Liese.

CENTER FOR BEAD RESEARCH, 4 Essex Street, Lake Placid, NY 12946. Telephone: (518) 523-1794. Director: Peter Francis, Jr.

CENTER FOR THE STUDY OF BEADWORK, P.O. Box 13719, Portland, OR 97213. Telephone: (503) 248-1848. Director: Alice Scherer. Quarterly newsletter ($20 a year for membership and 4 issues) gives listings of local bead societies, class listings around the country, reviews of new publications and articles. There is an up-to-date resource list ($1); library, study collection, slide bank.

SOCIETY OF BEAD RESEARCHERS, Membership: Lester Ross, P.O. Box 7304, Eugene, OR 97201; Publications Editor: Karlis Karklins, Parks Canada, 1600 Liverpool Court, Ottowa, Ontario, Canada KWA 0H3.

AUTHOR'S ACKNOWLEDGEMENTS

Many thanks to Steve Tanner and his assistant Ben Wood for taking great photographs; to Vicky Salter for her encouragement throughout, and to Jan Coxhill for her help with the weaving. Thanks also to Evelyn Cohen, Jean Growney and all the other contributors for allowing their work to be shown in the Gallery, and to Andrew Florides for the loan of the photograph of the Beadwork Cushion on page 31.

INDEX